Jewish Wisdom, a Modern Look

Jewish Wisdom, a Modern Look

(7000 Years of Continuous Evolution)

Asher Elkayam

To order additional copies of this book, contact:
Xlibris
1-888-795-4274
www.Xlibris.com
Orders@Xlibris.com
778310

A Word from Dr. Ackerman (Israel's Best Seller) about This Project

For the past two decades I have been following the works of Asher Elkayam and very much appreciate his originality in clarifying complex issues in the spheres of Judaism, Christianity, and Islam. Asher's writing is interesting, and he bases his research on analysis of the sources and reaching clear and logical conclusions that give the reader cause to think.

I recommend taking a serious look at his enriching books and feel certain that the reader will also derive great benefit from his new book in which considerable thought and energy has been invested.

Dr. Adam Ackerman

Jerusalem

In memory of Jacques Elkayam, my beloved brother who recently left this world. Jacques had nothing but love for every human being

In memory of Solomon and Sima Elkayam, my beloved parents who always encouraged me to learn and grow

To the late David and Lee Renbaum, my beloved relatives who never stopped inspiring me

And to all my dear departed relatives and friends who taught me to love and respect my fellow person

This book is dedicated with love to all my dear family members and my cherished relatives and friends all over the world.

To the Reader's Attention

All biblical quotes have been given special attention and have been personally translated by this author.

For the most accurate translation, we have used our existing knowledge of the Hebrew Tannakh and Mishnah while validating the translation through various dictionaries including comprehensive Hebrew dictionaries (see bibliography).

Some transliterated names and nouns (from Hebrew to English) may carry a different spelling among historians and authors. For example, the last name of Joseph Karo is also spelled Caro. Chuppa (canopy, allusion to sacred wedding ceremony) can also be spelled chuppah. Rabbi Shimon is also spelled in different books as Simeon. Challah (sacred bread) is also spelled hallah.

The Mishanh is a vast field of ideas. This book does not aim to cover all the 6,200 pages of the Mishnah, but it does concentrate on the essence and the wisdom derived from it.

Most mishanic rules cited in this book have been compared to today's way of life. This is what this project is about.

Finally, several names are intentionally repeated because they were represented in different chapters for different reasons. For example, Rabbi Yehuda Hanasi's quotes of wisdom were separated from the notes on his remarkable task in assembling the Mishnah. Also, the name of Rabbi Yohanan Ben Zakkai can be found in several chapters because of his ability to revolutionize and change the practice of Judaism.

Contents

Chapter Nine: Nashim (On Women), Third Order of the Mishnah

Chapter Twelve: Toharot(Purities), Sixth Order of the Mishnah) 162

Introduction

Noah, a God-fearing person, some seven thousand years ago, was chosen by God to preserve and prolong human life before the historic deluge covered the earth and drowned its inhabitants and all creatures. Enoch was quoted early on in the Bible as a righteous man and a God-fearing person. Before the advent of any biblical commandments, there has always been a divine guiding force, which ruled the earth.

The "do not kill" commandment existed since Adam and Eve. We know the story of Cain and Abel and the meaning of sacrifices to God. God rejected Cain's offering, which drove him to a point of committing a crime by killing his brother Abel.

The Bible does not give a detailed account on people who lived for hundreds of years between Adam and Abraham, except for citing their ages and their generations.

Some four thousand years ago, Abraham discovered God or maybe the Lord called on Abraham to reveal to humanity the presence of an almighty God.

Exact rules of behavior were not clearly spelled out until the arrival of Moses and the Ten Commandments.

Despite the fact that the laws of Hammurabi preceded Moses and despite the fact that some laws of Moses resemble the laws of Hammurabi, there is no comparison between the two sets of laws. The most similar laws between those of Hammurabi and the Hebrew Bible are laws about crime and punishment, which can be ruled in any culture. For example, the "eye for an eye" punishment did exist before Moses. However, the Bible of Moses encompasses hundreds of items not mentioned in the code of Hammurabi. The Talmud in this book will clarify further the rules of the Torah.

According to Bible scholars, among them Maimonides, there are 613 commandments in the Bible. In comparing the laws governing relations between people found in the Laws of Moses and the laws of Hammurabi, we find an immense difference between the two laws. For example, in the books of Exodus, Deuteronomy, and especially in the book of Leviticus, we find precise laws concerning priesthood, purification, the Holy Ark, the Sabbath, pure animals, idolatry, and many more laws not found anywhere else in the prehistoric legal system. Incidentally, the laws of Hammurabi concerning loss of animals mention the pig as a stolen animal among other animals, which should be returned to the original owner in any form, including monetary compensation. The pig, as we know, is an impure animal for the Israelites. Biblical laws forbid the consumption and (even) contact with that animal. For the record, Jews and Moslems observe the biblical dietary laws.

We shall examine hereby the laws of Moses and how they evolved through generations. We shall see how scholars interpreted the rules of the Torah and how they arrived to a near-perfect understanding of the scriptures.

Biblical prophets were among the best gatekeepers of the Torah. While many biblical kings often committed transgressions, the prophets were there to exhort the Israelites to repent and return to God in observing the Torah.

When prophecy dwindled down in the history of the Holy Land, there came the era of the Mishnah and Gemarah, otherwise called the Talmud. Following the Talmudic period (200 BCE to 500 CE and beyond), there have been numerous scholars and Bible interpreters who enriched the meaning of the Torah.

We shall concentrate in this project on the sources of the Jewish heritage and we shall give special emphasis to the Talmud and the Ethics of the Fathers, otherwise called Pirkey Avot or *Avot* in short, which, in itself, is a synopsis of the Mishnah. It summarized hundreds of interpretations and conclusions reached by talmudic and Mishnaic scholars on biblical laws and leaders like Moses, Joshua, King David and his psalms, King Solomon and his proverbs. We also find quotes from biblical prophets, judges, and poets. Subsequently, the Great Assembly and the elders who received the Torah used many quotes from the Bible to make their point, as we shall see further.

We shall see below how the Jewish culture never vanished. Better yet, the Jewish people survived throughout history thanks to their preserving the

Torah (which includes the Old Testament and its various interpretations) throughout the centuries.

The genial effort of postbiblical scholars to understand and interpret the scriptures has been an ongoing process, which has made Judaism one of the most resilient religions and enduring cultures in history.

We shall also examine how Jewish scholars and Bible interpreters emerged throughout history, thus giving a vernacular and modern interpretation to the rules of the Torah.

ABRAHAM, THE FATHER OF MONOTHEISM

"Abraham Journeying into the Land of Canaan" *by Gustave Doré*

Gen 12:1 Now the Lord had said unto Abram, Get thee out of thy country, and from thy kindred, and from thy father's house, unto a land that I will shew thee....

Chapter One

The Jewish Heritage

The Comeback Israelite

Have we wondered, What do we know or what do we think we know today as practicing and nonpracticing Jews on how we got here?

First, we must address the phenomenon of the "comeback Israelite" culture and its survival throughout the ages.

Jews were Israelites first before they were called Jews. The title *Jews* was derived from the tribe of Judah. In the scriptures, we learn that God preferred the house of Judah, which was started by King David because of his loyalty to the Lord.

In the book of Kings, we witness the forgotten Israelite culture, which made a comeback after one of the last kings, King Josiah, discovered the last book of Moses, the book of Deuteronomy, in 622 BCE.

After the destruction of the first Temple by Nebuchadnezzar (586 BCE), the Israelite and Hebrew culture flourished in Babylonia and resurged in the Holy Land some thirty years later when the Jews were allowed by King Cyrus to rebuild their temple in Jerusalem.

After the destruction of the second temple (70 CE), the Holy Land was physically destroyed, but not spiritually beaten. Rabban Yohanan Ben Zakkai, who managed to get out of Jerusalem despite its being besieged by the Romans, created the famous Academy of Yabneh (Yavneh). Thanks to him, the teaching of the Torah, which was forbidden in Jerusalem by the occupying powers, continued in other parts of the Holy Land. He also designed prayers to replace the traditional sacrifices to the Temple, which were done daily by the Israelites.

With his disciples and students, Rabbi Yohanan Ben Zakkai takes the most credit in reestablishing and prolonging the Jewish culture to the land of Israel and its people worldwide.

We shall visit this famous scholar and other eminent scholars like Rabbi Akiva (Akiba), Rabbi Shimon, Rabbi Meir, Rabbi Joshua, Rabbi Elazar, and several more brilliant sages when we analyze the Mishnah and Pirkey Avot below.

A few years after the destruction of the second temple by the Romans (70 CE), there was another rebellion, the Bar Kochbah (Bar Kokhba) rebellion, which protested the establishment of Roman culture in Jerusalem. That rebellion, which was conducted by Shimon Bar Kochbah in 135 CE, was unfortunately crushed but not without a giant loss to the Romans.

Even after the rebellion of Bar Kochbah, the spirit of Judaism survived in the Holy Land and out of the Holy Land in Babylonia. No more sacrifices were performed in Jerusalem. Instead, prayers and the study of the Torah flourished. The new practice of Judaism initiated earlier by Rabbi Yohanan reinforced the ethical encouragements of those biblical prophets who concentrated more on being righteous and just rather than offering sacrifices to the Lord.

This is the story of the eternal Jewish culture and Jewish spirit, which survived all ancient civilizations that have ceased to exist but are still mentioned today only in history books.

MOSES, THE LAWGIVER

"Moses Coming Down From Mt. Sinai" by Gustave Doré

Exo 32:15 And Moses turned, and went down from the mount, and the two tables of the testimony *were* in his hand: the tables *were* written on both their sides; on the one side and on the other *were* they written.

Chapter Two

The Torah, from One
Generation to the Other

For busy people who want to have a simple and clear idea on how we got here, here is a synopsis:

- We know that Moses gave the Torah (the five first books of the Hebrew Bible) to the Israelites. Whether or not we believe that the Ten Commandments were actually handed to Moses within two tablets by God Himself is immaterial for now. Whether or not we believe that the laws and precepts written in the Torah were actually dictated to Moses by God Himself should not be important to wonder about right now for the following reason: What is important is that the Ten Commandments and the ensuing Torah and the Tannakh (the entire Hebrew Bible) exist today, and they are a priceless gift to humankind, not just to the Jewish and the

Christian people but to other faiths, such as Islam and other faiths.

- We also know that after Moses died, Joshua took over his leadership culturally, strategically, and militarily, in order to get the children of Israel to their promised land.

- Following Joshua there were numerous prophets and leaders who took the name of judges who led and protected the children of Israel against its enemies, namely the Philistines (who were the immediate neighbors). The judges of Israel were more authoritative in their military power than in their legal power. A great example is Samson, who saved the Israelites from the hands of the Philistines, and Deborah (who was also a prophetess), who saved the Israelites from the hands of Sisera, the Canaanite commander who threatened the Israelites.

- The prophets represented a breath of fresh air for the lost Israelites who often forgot their God. Powerful prophets, such as Prophet Samuel, Prophet Isaiah, Prophet Jeremiah, and Prophet Ezekiel, were instrumental in leading the people spiritually and helping them return to their original heritage: God's Torah. Furthermore, they were practical in urging the people to concentrate on good deeds first before they performed sacrifices in Jerusalem.

- Under Prophet Samuel, Israel began to have a king. Whereas until then, the Israelites struggled with the idea of having God as their king, the idea of a human king became more and more evident following numerous protests by the Israelites, demanding a human king. King Saul was the very first king of Israel, followed by King David and King Solomon and many more kings. There were, in all, forty-two kings (including one queen).

- Unfortunately, the kingdom of the land of Israel split in two: north and south. The south was called Judah, and the north was called Israel. King David and his descendants ruled the kingdom of Judah. The kings of the north were considered wicked. According to the book of Kings, God preferred the kingdom of Judah because many southern kings followed God's rules and commandments.

- The kingdom of the Holy Land ended in 586 BCE after the destruction of the first Jerusalem temple, previously built by King Solomon. Most Israelites were exiled to Babylonia. This will bring us back to how our Jewish heritage was preserved.

- Historically, the Torah was given to the Israelites in the thirteenth century BCE. The temple of Solomon was built in the eighth century BCE and destroyed some three centuries later (historians differ on the exact duration of the temple). Nevertheless, its destruction by the Babylonians is agreed on by all historians to be (as we saw above) in the year 586 BCE on the ninth day of the Jewish month of Av.

- We need to emphasize as we move toward the preservation of the Torah that, during the reign of one of last kings, King Josiah (640–609 BCE), one of the books of Moses was found. It is believed to be the book of Deuteronomy. Until then, the Israelites and their kings were missing the warnings made by Moses to the Israelites, especially of chapter 28 of Deuteronomy. That discovery seemed to revolutionize the Israelite culture and faith, which was, until then, deplorable.

- Under King Josiah, belief in God and biblical religious rituals and customs were restored. Even the Passover holiday, which had been forgotten by many kings, was officially observed and solemnly reinstated while a massive purification of the temple and other holy venues took place.

- In Babylonia, where the exiled Jews gathered, the academies of Sura and Pumbedita flourished. Fortunately, the study and the interpretation of the Torah also took place in the Holy Land.

- This is how the Talmud Bavli (the Babylonian Talmud) and the Talmud Yerushalmi (the Jerusalem Talmud) developed. Jewish life and intensive study of the Torah continued in the Holy Land and in other cities than Jerusalem: Tiberias, Tsipori, Lydia, and other cities in the Holy Land.

- The Talmud Yerushalmi began to thrive after the Persians defeated the Babylonians (under

King Cyrus) and the Israelites returned to the Holy Land from their exile in Babylonia in 538 BCE.

- In the next chapter, we shall see how the study of the Torah evolved throughout the centuries.

Chapter Three

How the Torah Flourished throughout History

The following terms will be helpful in understanding how the Torah was enriched throughout the centuries.

- *Tannaim*, pronounced *tah-na-em*, were the teachers who studied and interpreted the Torah. *Tanna* (singular) is an Aramaic word for *learn* or *study.* The tannaim were present during the first two centuries of the Common Era. The tannaim were the teachers of the oral Torah, which includes the Mishnah.

- *Amoraim* (pronounced *a-mo-ra-eem*) were the post-Mishnaic teachers who are represented in the Gemarah, which is part of the Talmud.

- We begin to understand that the Mishnah preceded the Gemarah. The Mishnah is a legal discussion on the fundamentals of Jewish law. The Gemarah is the interpretation of the Mishnah using metaphors, examples, parables, and assumptions, leading to the understanding of the Mishnah. The Mishnah itself is another way of reading and understanding the basics of the Torah of Moses.

- From here, we go to learn two new terms: *Halakhah* and *Aggadah.* Halakhah is the legal discussion of the rabbis. The literal meaning of Halakhah is "to walk." Halakhah can be explained further by the way one should walk, behave, and live.

- From Halakhah we move to *Aggadah*, which is the nonlegal part of the rabbinic literature. Because it is nonlegal, it goes into lore and legend, and it completes the Halakhah, thus going hand in hand with it, leading to a better understanding of the legal Torah.

- The next three terms are in Aramaic. They are *Mekhilta*, *Sifra*, and *Siphre*. *Mechilta* means "measure," and it explains and comments on the book of Exodus. Sifra means "book," and it comments on the book of Leviticus (which has many laws on purity and rituals). Siphre means "the books," and it comments on the books of Numbers and Deuteronomy.

- *Midrash* is the next term. *Midrashim* (plural of Midrash was the term used for the sages to discuss and understand the laws of the Torah. Midrash means "search" or "inquiry." The word Midrash originates in the three-letter word *D-R-SH*, from which the word *drash* or *drasha* is translated into *inquiry.* From that, we also have two words to understand some verses of the Torah: *Drash* and *Pshat.* Drash would mean, in this case, "an explanation," and Pshat would be "a simple term without interpretation"—for example: do not kill, do not steal, and other similar commandments.

- The exiled scholars conducted endless debates and investigations in order to understand and illuminate further the meaning of the Torah.

- Now that we spoke about Halakhah and Aggadah and Midrashim, when we connect those terms, we come up with *Halakhic midrashim* and *Aggadic midrashim.* The

Aggadic midrashim definitely completes the more serious Halakhic midrashim because the Halakhic midrashim represents the law. We underline here that the Aggadic midrashim is the story and the legend.

- Tradition has told us numerous times that the Torah was not given only as a written scripture. The oral Torah accompanied the written Torah. The oral Torah had to be transmitted from generation to generation until it arrived to those sages we spoke about above, all the way to the *Geonim*. *Gaon* is the singular of Geonim. It stands for someone who was the head of an academy (like Sura) and is a learned spiritual leader in his generation.

- The interpretation of the Torah did not stop with the Tannaim and the Amoraim. The study of the Torah and its illumination continued throughout centuries all the way to today. We must praise those sages who made history after the departure of the classic Talmudists: Rashi, whose real name is Rabbi Shlomo Ben Itzhak (1040–1105 CE), was born in France. He was an erudite of the Torah and the

Talmud. He explained the hidden sides of the scriptures with clarity. Moses Maimonides or Rabbi Moshe Ben Maimon (1135–1204 CE) was a brilliant doctor, philosopher, and scholar who wrote, among other books, the *Mishneh Torah* (which represented an easier way to understand the Torah). Rashbam (1083–1174) was born in Northern France. He was considered the leading rabbi in medieval times. He was the grandson of Rashi. He also continued Rashi's work, having made additional interpretations on the books of Job and on the Song of Songs. Rabbenu Tam (1100–1171), another grandson of Rashi, was born in Ramerupt on the Seine River (France). He was a great *Tosaftist* (meaning a specialist in additions to the meaning of the Torah and Halakhah). He was considered one of the most illustrious Ashkenazi (European) rabbis who made their contribution to preserving and enhancing the meaning of the Torah. Yehuda Halevi (1075–1141) was born in medieval Spain and was the most prolific Jewish poet of his time.

- At a time when Judaism was attacked right and left by Christians and Moslems, Rabbi Yehuda Halevi found his answer to the religious world by composing his great work that he called the *Kuzari*. In the Kuzari book, he expressed his beliefs on how an entire kingdom of the Khazars converted to Judaism and how and why they converted. Abraham Ibn Ezra (1092–1167) was born in Tuleda, Spain. He was also a great poet and a friend of Yehuda Halevi. Unlike Yehuda Halevi, he specialized in Hebrew grammar and secular science such as astronomy and mathematics. His contribution to Judaism was so great that he was welcome in several countries, including Italy, England, Babylonia, and the Holy Land. His name is being frequently quoted in Jewish literature. Saadia Gaon (882–942) was born in Sura, Babylonia. He translated the entire Bible into Arabic. He used reason in order to interpret the Torah and Halakhah. He became the head of the academy of Sura. His works are still popular today, and they represent a source of Jewish wisdom and Jewish philosophy. Philo of Alexandria (20 BCE–40 CE) was a Jewish and a Greek scholar as well. He was inspired by Plato and other Greek philosophers. He tried in his many works to understand the concept of God and creation. Unlike the other scholars mentioned above, his philosophical works contributed to building the foundations for Christianity. We clarify here that many of the intellectual Jews in the Diaspora (exile of the Jews from the Holy Land to other countries—in this case, Egypt) were influenced by the Hellenistic culture, which dominated Egypt during the Roman occupation of the Middle East around the first century. Philo was considered the most brilliant Jewish scholar who could bridge between Judaism and Hellenism (see chapter 16 on the Christian connection to Judaism).

- Because there have been so many commentators and translators in Judaism following the medieval sages mentioned above, it will be almost impossible to list the hundreds of rabbis and luminaries who grasped the meaning of the Torah and the Talmud and made them available for those who wanted to know more in the twentieth and twenty-first century.

- Nevertheless, this chapter on those icons who made us understand the Torah and the Talmud could not be complete without mentioning two more sources of wisdom, which helped scholars understand the Talmud. At the end of the fifteenth century there rose in Italy Rabbi Obadiah Bartenora (1455–1520 CE) whose comments on the Torah and the Talmud became indispensable for Torah scholars everywhere. He fled from Spain to Italy and then on to the Holy Land (1488) where he became the chief rabbi of Jerusalem. He became the chief spiritual leader of the impoverished Jews of the Holy Land as well as of the Jews of the Diaspora.

- Another source of commentaries are *Ein Yaacov*, which is a compilation of commentaries by Jacob Ben Solomon Ibn Habib and his son Rabbi Levi Ibn Habib. Ibn Habib fled Spain in 1492, following the Spanish Inquisition, and settled in Salonika. His son, Rabbi Levi Ibn Habib, also fled from Portugal at the age of seventeen after he was forced to convert to Christianity. Both Rabbi Jacob and his son were instrumental in compiling the Talmud legends and commentaries. They made them look easy and simple for Jews who faced conversion to Christianity. Ein Yaacov was also a powerful tool against Jewish converts from Spain who criticized the Talmud and its legends. That masterpiece was more recently translated by Yaacov Abraham Finkel, a holocaust survivor who managed to enter the United States in 1942 and ended up living in Brooklyn, New York, until his death in 2016.

- The Shulchan Aruch is a prepared table of laws encompassing knowledge and simple rules of Jewish behavior and practice. All those rules are based on the Torah. It is another way of keeping Jewish customs and rituals alive. Yoseph Caro established the Shulhan Aruch for early Sephardic populations. Based on his work, Rabbi Isserles and other scholars summarized and added to it more rules of the Torah, making them comprehensible to the average person.

- *Hoshen Mishpat* is an additional version of Shulchan Aruch, and it concerns legal and judicial matters in the Jewish law (see chapter 4, on Shulhan Aruch).We should add that Moses Maimonides initiated another way of keeping in touch with the dispersed Jews worldwide. He was the initiator of the *responsa.* The responsa was a question-answer type, which was designed for those Jews in the Diaspora who needed an answer to their religious question (some of those communities were located at a distance from Spain, for example, in Yemen). Furthermore, thanks to those scholars, people in the Diaspora could ask questions and get an answer for their questions. We must credit Maimonides for writing on this subject. He clarified religious situations in writing another very important book called *The Guide to the Perplexed* (*Moreh Nevuchim*). The need to do that was urgent as some Jews under Muslim rules were forced to pray with Muslims. Maimonides was instrumental in advising Jews to cooperate with Muslims without losing their Jewish identity (see chapter 5 for further comments of the responsa).

- The understanding of the Torah does not end in the Mishnah, Talmud, responsa, or Shulhan Aruch. Jewish scholars also developed what we call the *Zohar* or kabbalah, which is Jewish mysticism. In fact, *kabbalah* means "receiving." It is the inspiration received by the spirit of God to a person, man or woman. This is a very different chapter to discuss. The *Zohar*, which was inspired and initiated by Rabbi Shimon Bar Yohai and his son, is another way of looking at the Jewish heritage and can be discussed in a future project. After Rabbi Shimon, many more scholars received that inspiration and followed up on it. Moses de Leon, of Spain (1240-1305) is known as a major scholar in Jewish mysticism.

- Jews and non-Jews alike study the *Zohar*, which could not be comprehended by the average faithful because of its abstract and superspiritual nature. Finally, the complexity of the Zohar is that it aims at striving to reach out to God through spiritual and mystical phases, which must be reached step-by-step. No wonder that the *Zohar* was called Jewish mysticism.

- In today's twenty-first century, we can appreciate how mishnaic and postmishnaic scholars worked at preserving the Hebrew and Jewish cultural heritage. Jewish studies and Jewish history are taught today all over the US as well as all over the world where there are Jewish communities. We can also credit spiritual leaders and rabbis all over the world who contributed so much to the preservation of the Jewish customs and rituals, beginning with the circumcision all the way to the bar/bat mitzvah to the chuppah (sacred Jewish wedding) and the solemn observance of many Jewish holidays, such as the high holidays, namely Rosh Hashanah and Yom Kippur.

- The Sabbath is considered by the Bible and the Talmud as the most important holy day. It is celebrated worldwide in synagogues and Jewish temples as a special day which surpasses all holidays. Other important festivals like Passover and Shavuot are tied to the exodus of Egypt, and they are observed. Other holidays like Hanukkah, Purim, and the fifteenth of the month Shevat (Arbor Day) are also observed in our time.

Chapter Four

The Shulhan Aruch—a Prepared Table

Simplified Rules to Observe

Following the study of the Torah of Moses (the Pentateuch) and the rest of the Tannakh (the Old Testament) came the Mishnaic and Talmudic studies. Eminent rabbis and scholars, inspired by the Talmud, assembled the laws of the Torah and simplified them in order to help the average person understand the abovenamed studies. The method on which those simplified laws were based was called Shulhan Aruch. The latter actually means "a prepared table." For a further explanation, it is a simplification and modern interpretation of the rules of the Torah. The basic Bible of Moses was given with many concise rules. Some of them were often too complex to understand.

Following many deliberations, debates, discussions, and interpretations, the abovementioned scholars came out with rules, which became easier to understand.

Since the most important things in Judaism are studying the Torah, praying, performing good deeds, caring for the poor and the deprived, establishing justice, honoring parents, and observing the Sabbath, the following list summarizes the principles of the Shulhan Aruch.

Basic Rules of the Shulhan Aruch

The following principles are based on Joseph Karo (1488–1575), Rabbi Moses Isserles (1530–1572), and other scholars who based their rules on the way they interpreted the commandments found in the Pentateuch.

On Judges

- A judge must be extremely serious in his work. An unjust verdict can be compared to hell.

- A judge should be humble and treat poor or rich people the same way.

- A judge should also be busy doing other work than that concerning the law itself.

- Dignity must be strictly kept at the office of the judge.

- In all, no person should be appointed as a judge because of his money or wealth.

- A judge cannot make a legal mistake (refer to Pirkey Avot for more on judges, justice, and law).

On Dignity in a Synagogue

- There is a difference between a synagogue and a house of study.

- Whereas you cannot eat or sleep in a synagogue, you are permitted to do so in a house of study.

- One may not conduct business in a synagogue unless that business is for religious studies.

- Special attention must be given to people's clothes when they enter a synagogue: the body and head must be covered.

- It is permitted to sell an old synagogue in ruins when a new synagogue has been built.

- Dignity, respect, and sanctity apply to a ruined synagogue just as to a new synagogue.

- We cannot build apartments on top of a synagogue except for a room expressly built for religious purposes.

Obligation to Study the Torah (Rabbi Moses Isserles's Notes on Joseph Karo)

- Every Jew, rich or poor, must study the Torah.

- Supporting the study of the Torah is equivalent to its study.

- In emergency (only), the prayer of the Shema (Hear, O Israel) can take place instead of a lengthy study.

- Study the Torah before getting married.

- The study of the Torah is divided in three parts: Torah, Mishnah, and Talmud.

- It is permitted to study other sciences as long as they do not include heretical subjects.

- It is permitted to study the cabala (kabbalah) only after completing the classical studies (the Torah and its interpretation).

- It is permitted to teach the Bible for a fee. This does not apply to the oral Torah (see clarification ahead).

- Women get rewarded for studying the Torah even as they are not required to study it.

- Bring an "unworthy" pupil to the right path before you teach him.

- Study only with a righteous rabbi. A great sage who is not righteous should be avoided.

- A rabbi should never be angry with slow pupils. He should pursue his teaching with those who are slow to absorb until they reach their learning point.

- Pupils should never be ashamed to ask questions. They should ask questions until they understand.

- A rabbi has the right to be angry with his pupils only if they are lazy or unwilling to learn.

- Questions to the rabbi should be made only after he has entered the house of study and settled down.

- No more than three questions on a certain topic should be made to the rabbi (in our time, it is not unusual to ask multiple questions).

- Rabbis are obliged to reply only to relevant questions (this may not be acceptable in our century).

- The reply to a question made by a sage precedes that of a pupil (that rule may not apply anymore in the twenty-first century).

- One should never sleep in a house of study unless that person has no other place to sleep following the study.

- Speak only of the Torah in the house of study. Exclude any foreign (non-Torah) subjects.

- The study of the Torah is greater than a good deed although the Torah prescribes doing a good deed. In Pirkey Avot, some sages taught the opposite. Doing good deeds exceeds the study of the Torah, in the Mishnah and Pirkey Avot.

- Work, in order to make a living, must accompany the study of the Torah. Although the oral Torah does not permit to make a living out of the study of the Torah, it is normal for the community to economically support the spiritual leader and the educational scholars.

- Studying in loud voice is preferred to studying silently.

- Study of the Torah is done more in the long nights of the fall and winter. One should make the most effort to study in the shorter nights of the summer. Therefore, our sages declared the fifteenth day of the month of Av to begin the nightly study of the Torah (this rule is found in the Mishnah).

- Whenever a Torah scholar completes a tractate of the Talmud, a religious feast is observed.

Respect for Scholars and Aged People in the Shulhan Aruch

- Respect is equally important to the aged as it is to the learned people even if they are young.

- Rise before an aged person or a scholar except if they are in a bathhouse.

- Workmen are exempt from rising before the sages (obviously because they are busy doing their daily work).

- Older heathens are entitled to the same respect given to the rabbis. A person famous for good deeds is entitled to the same respect the aged people get.

- Special respect is to be given to the head of the court, such as Hillel the Great, who was considered second to the prince. The prince spoken about is Rabbi Yehuda (Yehudah)

Hanassi, who labored for years to compile all the orders of the Mishnah.

- When the chief rabbi enters the college, all rise until he asks them to sit down (the same goes for a dean, head scholar, or chief judge). This respectful gesture, an old American tradition, still exists in Europe.

- An older person is entitled to more respect than a sage who is not outstanding in learning.

Orah Hayyim, Another Interpretation of the Shulhan Aruch, concerning Passover.

- Kiddush (blessing on the wine) always starts at dark, on the eve of the holiday of Passover.

- Rich and poor should recline during the Seder.

- Reclining is always on the left side. Mishnaic sages have opposing opinions on this subject.

- Women are exempt from reclining.

- Note on reclining: Rabbi Karo follows the Spanish tradition of reclining. The other version of Shulhan Aruch is of Rabbi Isserles, who does not require reclining in the Passover Seder.

- The four cups of wine must be consumed during the Passover Seder.

- Even those who usually do not drink wine must do so in Passover (in modern times, people who are allergic to wine or are reluctant to consume wine may simply have a taste of the wine or substitute it with grape juice).

- Red wine is preferred to white wine during the Passover Seder.

- The Passover wine consumption is for all: men, women, children, and the needy people (who are provided for by the community).

Rabbi Solomon Ganzfried (1804–1886) and His Version of Shulhan Aruch

Rabbi Ganzfried published his own Shulhan Aruch on harmful words.

- It is a worse offense to wrong with words than to wrong someone in buying and selling.

Wronging women with words is especially incorrect as women are very sensitive.

- Example of wronging someone in words: deceiving, misleading, saying something and meaning something else.

- If a person has repented for wrongdoing, that person should be forgiven.

- It is wrong to call a man by a nickname he hates (in modern times, we must apply the same principle to all people).

- It is wrong to "steal" someone's heart. An example of that is to deceive a buyer of meat by not disclosing the exact way the meat was slaughtered.

- A person should not invite someone to his table if he knows well that that someone will refuse to come.

Yalkut Yoseph

It is important to state that many other rabbis and scholars published their own Shulhan Aruch (prepared table) as they adapted their understanding of the Torah to their generations and congregations. A good example is *Yalkut Yoseph*, written by a chief rabbi in Israel: Itzhak Yoseph, the son of the deceased Rabbi Obadiah Yoseph (1920–2013). The latter was an authority in Halakhah, Jewish law, and observance of the Torah in Israel. He was a precocious learner. He was born in Iraq in 1920. In 1924, he immigrated to Israel with his parents. He became one the most gifted and talented Sephardic scholars. He was also a *posek*, meaning the ultimate decider on a biblical ruling that may have doubt among religious rabbinical judges.

Rabbi Yoseph was so influential in Israel that he managed to mobilize political forces in Israel and around the world in order to bring the lost Ethiopian Jews to Israel. It was not without a superhuman effort that the Jews of Ethiopia were finally flown to the Holy Land while civil war was still raging in Ethiopia. Operation Moses in 1984 and Operation Solomon in 1991 completed the massive wave of immigration of the Ethiopian Jews to Israel.

Chapter Five

Maimonides, Shulhan Aruch, and Responsa

Although Rabbi Moshe Ben Maimon lived long before Rabbi Yoseph Karo and Rabbi Isserles, he had his own set of laws. Maimonides lived between 1135 CE and 1204 CE. He was brilliant in the Golden Era of Spain, and he combined the knowledge of the Torah with that of medicine and philosophy. Here are some rules Maimonides taught us and taught scholars after him:

- Maimonides explains the last commandment of the Torah: "Your shall not covet" (Exodus 20:14). His explanation is as follows: You may desire or covet someone else's property (in your mind), but a penalty comes only if you pressure or trick the owner of any property even if he does not want to sell it.

- On charity, Maimonides stresses that charity is a must for everyone and should be a way of life. He quotes Isaiah 1:27 and Genesis 18:19.

- No one becomes poor by giving charity.

- Not giving charity is wicked.

- When you give, give cheerfully.

- Never offend a poor person.

- A charity fundraiser for the poor is a great way to perform a mitzvah (a good deed).

- The highest degree of charity is to help a poor person to become economically independent.

- The lowest degree of charity is to give grudgingly or with disdain.

- Another way of giving charity is to hire orphans and widows.

- On the other hand, it is wrong to endanger yourself to perform charity in order to claim self-pride.

- Maimonides also wrote responsas. The responsas were written to Jews, non-Jews, and converts to Judaism.

- A convert wanted to know if Moslems were idolaters: Maimonides's answer was that the Moslems (Muslims) were not idolaters. However, before Islam was established as the true religion of Moslems, their ancestors worshiped three gods: Peor, Mercury, and Kemosh.

Other Responsas by Other Sages

The method of written answers by Maimonides gave way to other rabbis and scholars to help clarify and respond to religious questions in their generations:

- Rabbi Yom Tov Ben Avraham Ishbili, commonly known by his Hebrew acronym Ritba, lived between 1260 and 1320. He was the famous Spanish Talmudist of the fourteenth century. He lived some two hundred years after Maimonides, and he was instrumental in giving responsas to Jewish people and scholars who needed help in their understanding of the Torah.

- Rabbi Yair Hayyim Bacharach (1639–1702) was a prominent rabbi in his time. He also provided answers. One of his famous responsas was about luck and lottery. He used Talmudic cases in order to support his version that there is an element of divine guidance in luck and lottery.

Conclusion on Shulhan Aruch and Responsas

The above rules and responsas, which guided the Jewish people in understanding the laws of Judaism, represented a continuation of Talmudic and Mishnaic debates found in the Talmud (Mishnah and Gemarah). They arrived at plausible situations without contradicting the spirit of the Torah of Moses.

The wisdom of the Talmudic era, including a special tractate of Pirkey Avot (the Wisdom of the Fathers) to be found below in this project, led to new generations of sages.

We have mentioned above the sages who made a remarkable impression on the development and interpretation of Judaism. The list of Jewish sages and rabbis who emerged throughout history is endless. Nevertheless, both Sephardic (from Spain) and Ashkenazi(originating from the rest of Europe) scholars kept the tradition of interpreting the Torah and Halakhah in a manner that did not antagonize the original laws of the Torah of Moses.

KING SOLOMON, THE WISEST OF ALL MEN

"Solomon" *by Gustave Doré*

2Ch 1:11 And God said to Solomon, Because this was in thine heart, and thou hast not asked riches, wealth, or honour, nor the life of thine enemies, ... Wisdom and knowledge is granted unto thee....

Chapter Six

Introduction to the Talmud

The Talmud includes the Mishnah and the Gemarah. The Mishnah means "study" or "repeat," and also means "learn repeatedly." According to tradition, the oral Torah was given together with the written Torah by God to Moses when he received the Ten Commandments. The Gemarah is the explanation and the clarification of the Mishnah by hundreds of scholars who lived before and after the first millennium.

While the Mishnah explains the Torah of Moses, the Gemarah interprets through debates and reasoning parables the contents of the Mishnah.

From the Torah to the Talmud

The oral Torah was transmitted from generation to generation since the time of Moses (1313 BCE). Rabbis, scholars, and simple worshipers had to rely on their memory in order to learn and discuss its contents. Although numerous writings existed on the oral Torah, there was no written book of the Mishnah until it was assembled by one of the most illustrious scholars in the second century CE, Rabbi Yehudah Hanasi (Judah the Prince). The assembling of the Mishnah took some forty years, between the years 140 CE and 200 CE.

After the Mishnah was available to rabbis, teachers, and students, the need to understand its meaning and debate its contents became necessary. This is how the second part of the oral Torah, the Gemarah, was created.

The Gemarah had two versions: the Palestinian Gemarah (or Jerusalem Gemarah) and the Babylonian Gemarah. The Palestinian Gemarah was written in Western Aramaic, while the Babylonian Gemarah was written in Eastern Aramaic.

The authors of the Mishnah were called *Tanaim* (*ta-nah-eem*), and the authors of the Gemarah were the *Amoraim* (*a-mo-ra-eem*). When something had to be added to the Gemarah from outside sources, it was called Beraita (*beh-rye-ta*). When some material was added to the Gemarah, it was called Tosefta.

The Gemarah and the Mishnah are called Talmud, in short. Talmud means "study" or "learning."

The Palestinian Talmud was completed between 350 CE and 400 CE. The Babylonian Talmud was completed around the year 500 CE.

The Mishnah contained biblical, religious, and legal matters. Those legal matters took the name of Halakhah (meaning "the way the law goes"). The Gemarah also contained legal matters (Halakhah), but it also contained *Aggadah* (legendary or lore stories) in order to elucidate the Mishnah.

When time arose to inquire about something, it was called Midrash (inquiry). Therefore, there were Halakhic midrashim (legal inquiries) and Aggadic midrashim (legendary inquiries).

It is worthwhile to note that most biblical scholars agree that the Torah, which was transmitted orally from generation to generation for seven centuries, was finally recorded on a long Torah scroll. The Torah scroll is made of panels of parchment made from the cured hides of a kosher animal (sheep or cow). The panels are carefully sewn together to form a long scroll.

The Torah scroll is written without vowels. It must be carefully hand copied by a specialized scribe who could not make a single mistake. Thus, we learn how every single word in the Torah must be taken seriously.

At the time of Ezra the Scribe, the Torah was finally recorded and organized so it could be read to the Israelites. Ezra the Scribe made the Torah available to the average person during the fifth century BCE or, more precisely, during the third quarter of that century.

Structure of the Talmud

The Talmud, which includes the Mishnah and the Gemarah, consists of 6 orders (chapters or parts) and 63 tractates (sub chapters) and contains over 6,200 pages.

The Palestinian Talmud was redacted by Rav Muna and Rav Yosi (Rabbi Yosi) around the year 350 CE. Although it was called the Jerusalem Talmud, it was written and redacted outside Jerusalem in

Tiberias and Cesarea. Why so? Because Jerusalem was destroyed by the Romans in the year 70 CE, and its scholars were forbidden to promote the Torah in Jerusalem.

Between the year 70 CE and year 350 CE a lot happened to the Jewish life and culture in the Holy Land. As seen earlier, the Palestinian Talmud was completed in the year 350 CE, some twenty-five years after Constantine the emperor declared Jerusalem as the holy city of Christianity in 325 CE.

Consequently, the Jewish culture and way of life began to weaken. What is more, in the year 425 CE, under Theodosius, the Jewish patriarch, the traditional *nasi* (prince) ceased to exist in the Holy Land. With it, rabbinical ordination, called *Semicha*, was suspended.

On the other hand, the Babylonian Talmud continued to thrive. It was more concise than the Palestinian Talmud, and it survived and thrived for another two hundred years.

Similarities and Differences between the Jerusalem Talmud and the Babylonian Talmud

- Both Talmud's cover the Mishnah.

- Both Talmud's were limited only to thirty-seven of the sixty-three tractates of the Mishnah.

- The Jerusalem Talmud covered the subject of *zeraim* (seeds) and agricultural matters, which was limited to the land of Israel only.

- The Babylonian Jews could not cover the ritual of sacrifice in Babylonia while it was forbidden in the land of Israel. The corresponding order to the sacrifices was called *kodashim* (holy rituals).

- Both Talmuds deal with six large orders of the Mishnah. Since both deal with the same orders (*Sedarim*), we shall examine below those orders and their meanings.

As indicated earlier, the Mishnah is divided into six orders. They are six large chapters with multiple subchapters called tractates *masekhot*). Some long tractates encompass various subjects we have called subtractates for simplicity.

They are accompanied by multiple explanations of the Gemarah, the Jerusalem Gemarah and the Babylonian Gemarah.

Discussions, agreements, disagreements, and decisions are made in commenting on the rules of the Torah and the meanings behind its commandments.

As we shall see in the upcoming orders and tractates, the Torah will have a richer meaning as it is discussed, debated on, and dissected by the sages and the scholars of the Talmudic era.

Within the sixty-three tractates in the Mishnaic chapters, Pirkey Avot is considered the sixty-third tractate. It is a long tractate, and it covers several rules and opinions about legality, ethics, morality, and justice. Avot is found in the order of *Nezikin*, and it is in the second-to-the-last tractate in that order.

ONE PAGE FROM TRACTATE ONE: BERAKHOT

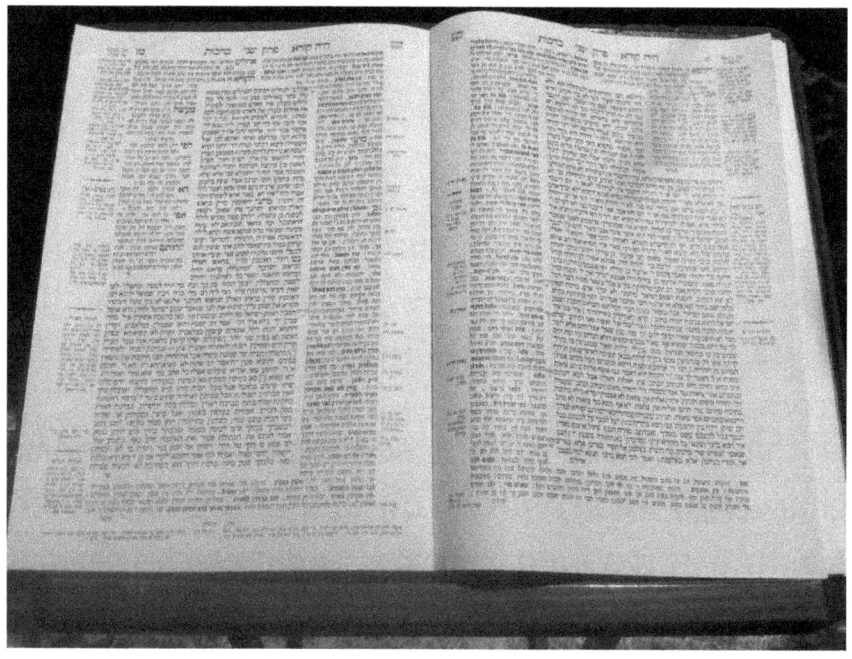

Chapter Seven

ZERAIM (Pronounced Zeh-Rah-Eem)

First Order of the Mishnah

The order Zeraim (seeds) deals with agricultural matters, concentrating on the seventh year of the land and the tithes to be given to the temple. The seventh year of the land is called the *Shemitah* (meaning "rest" or "let alone"). This is the seventh year for the land to be left alone. It is forbidden to use the land for cultivating or seeding as prescribed by the Bible.

Zeraim deals also with the commandment of the tithes. Every Israelite is to contribute the tithe of his produce, harvest, and cattle.

Besides the tithe, it is prescribed that every Israelite brings to the temple the first fruit on the festival of the first fruit called *Shavuot*, which falls forty-nine days after the festival of Passover.

Tractate 1. Berakhot or blessings, pronounced *beh-ra-khot*, is when the sages discuss the earliest time that the prayer of *Shema* (Hear, O Israel) should be recited. They came out with the deadline of midnight but extended it to dawn as a fence to the Torah. They also debated about what time of day (or night) should the story of the Exodus be read. They also debated about the concentration in prayer. Recitation of the Shema without deep concentration and devotion does not count. While reciting the Shema, a man may salute another man while praying without interrupting the prayer.

Women, slaves, and minors are exempt from reciting the Shema, but they are not exempt from the regular prayer, called *tefillah*, and things such as affixing a mezuzah at the front door or making a blessing after meals. Women are exempt because of their family duties and responsibilities while minors are still too young to assume responsibility in prayer.

The reader might notice a slight confusion here as it said earlier that women are obligated to perform the tefillah (prayer). Later on, it says that they are exempt because of their duties, including household work and raising a family. Women may make their own prayer, and it does not have to be in a congregation. In conservative synagogues worldwide, especially in the US, women assume religious duties just as men do.

Discussion also took place if women counted in the proper quorum to recite the blessing after meal. The tefillah is the real prayer (morning and evening), and it should be done in extreme devotion without any distraction.

Our sages also discussed and agreed that different prayers should be recited for different kinds of fruit, whether it is fruit of the tree (apple), fruit of the vine (wine), or fruit of the earth (potato).

In this tractate, we find the usual arguments between the House of Hillel and the House of Shammai concerning the *havdalah* (the prayer recited Saturday night at the end of the Sabbath). Most sages agree with the House of Hillel who said that the blessings should follow this order: the blessing over the lamp (candles today), the spices, the food, and the havdalah itself. The havdalah is a short prayer praising God for discerning between a holy day (the Sabbath) and a regular day.

In synagogues today, the prayers are respectively about light (lighting candles, making a blessing over the wine, smelling spices and saying a prayer of the havdalah. The lighting of the candles and the smelling of the spices are forbidden during the entire Sabbath, which begins Friday night at sundown.

Tractate 2. Peah, pronounced *peh-ah*, means "corner," relating to the corner of the field to be untouched after the harvest. It is left for the poor and the needy. The rabbis extended the Peah not only to grain but also to various types of fruit and various types of grain. It is also prescribed by the Torah in Deuteronomy 14:22–23. In order to create a fence around the commandment of the Peah (corner of the field), the rabbis established that the amount of harvest left in the field should not be less than the sixth of the total produce of the field. The poor may make three searches each day, allowing the women and the elderly to have more chances to glean leftover harvest.

Rabbi Akiva defended the poor and the owner as well. He was in the opinion that anything dropped from the sickle while properly harvesting belonged to the poor. However, anything dropped through what we call today a mechanical malfunction, like two sickles banging each other and dropping sheaves of grain on the soil, belong to the owner.

Tractate 3. Demai (doubt), pronounced de-may, is related to bringing the tithe to the temple. It is thoroughly discussed in this section. The duty of bringing the tithe is a serious matter. It is also discussed in the book of Avot. Any miscalculation of the exact measure of the tithe could bring calamity to the word (see chapter on Pirkey Avot, page 272). The word *demai* is a Talmudic word that translates into "doubt." There should be no doubt left between those who contribute the tithe and those who receive it. The word *demai* is also close to the word *dimion,* which also means "imagination" and also means "false belief," a word carried for thousands of years and retained by many practicing Jews worldwide, including the Jews of Morocco (of which this author is personally familiar with).

In that same section, the sages of the Talmud assembled the most important biblical laws of behavior a man should follow daily or timely, namely, "leaving the corner of the field for the poor (peah)," "bringing the first fruit to the temple (*Bikkurim*), "performing the commandment of pilgrimage to the temple (*reayon*—pronounced *reh-ah-yon*)," and "studying the Torah (Talmud Torah)" (Peah 1:1).

In a further discussion of the Talmudic rabbis, it is said that "these are the things which bring enjoyment to a person in this world while the capital is saved for the world to come. They are: honoring father and mother, deeds of loving kindness, making peace between a man and his fellow person, and the study of the Torah is equal to them all" (Peah 1:1).

This summary of good deeds is repeated in daily prayers in synagogues worldwide with certain additions such as giving hospitality to strangers, concentrating in prayer, visiting the sick, honoring the bride, accompanying the dead to his (or her) last destination, bringing peace not only between man and man but also between man and wife, and studying the Torah, which is equal to them all.

Tractate 4. Kilayeem (diverse kinds)—pronounced *keel-ah-yeem*—refers to mixing animals of different breeds for work or breeding or wearing clothes of different fabrics like wool and linen. The Bible does not give a special reason why it is forbidden, but (as in every religion), there are laws, which are observed without questioning.

Rabbi Akiva permits the grafting of vegetables from the same family, like onions and wild onions. Rabbi Judah's opinion to have a vegetable grafted to a tree was not accepted. The Bible says on this matter, "You shall not sow your vineyard with a different kind of seed . . . you shall not plow with an ox and ass together. You shall not wear garment combining wool and linen together" (Deuteronomy 22:9–11).

On this matter, the Mishnah reports on Kilayeem 9:8 that "only spun and woven fabrics are forbidden under the law of diverse kinds." Rabbi Shimon Ben Elazar says, "The verse means that he who wears *shaatnez* [mixed cloths of different fabrics] is estranged and estranges his Father in Heaven against him."

The Mishnah in Kilayeem 9: 2 says, "Silk and coarse silk are not included in the law of diverse kinds, but they are still forbidden because of their appearance. Mattresses and cushions do not come under the law of diverse kinds, provided a man's flesh does not contact them directly."

We can see how the mixing of breeds and fabrics was taken so seriously by the Bible and by the Talmudic sages.

In modern times, that law of mixing fabrics and vegetables is not strictly followed because of modern scientific research and development leading to safe-eating vegetables (like mixing cauliflower and broccoli and other clothing materials made of different fabrics causing no harm to humans).

Tractate 5. Sheviit—pronounced *she-vee-eet*—represents the seventh year when the land is subject to total rest. Number seven is so important to Jewish law since God created heaven and earth in six days and rested on the seventh day. There are some exceptions in regard to working the land on the seventh year. The Talmud says, "Newly plowed land may be rented in the seventh year from a non-Jew but not from a Jew. Non-Jews may be encouraged when they labor in the fields in the seventh year" (Sheviit 3:8).

Another important aspect of the shemitah was the *prozbul,* which was a new law established by Rabbi Hillel and was meant to secure loans repayments even after the end of the sixth year. This discouraged people from making short-term loans close to the end of the seventh year without any intention of repaying them. Hillel quoted the last book of the Pentateuch in order to justify the law of the prozbul as it said in Deuteronomy,

"Beware lest something will be in your heart, saying, 'The seventh year of remission is approaching' and you become mean to your poor kinsman, giving him nothing. He will cry out [on you] to the Lord and you become guilty. You should surely give him and have no regrets for, by doing so, the Lord will bless you in all what you do in all and in your occupation" (Deuteronomy 15:9–10).

As Rabbi Hillel chose verse 9 of chapter 15, verse 10 reinforces his position in imposing the law of the prozbul.

Tractate 6. Terumot, free-will offering (pronounced *the-roo-mot)*, is another part of this Zeraim section. This offering is not required from a minor or a non-Jew or a mentally challenged person. Everyone is required to contribute a portion of his (or her) grain, oil, fruit, and wine.

The rabbis argued whether or not an offering could be given to the temple if it was defiled. This could mean that an unclean person could defile an offering by touching it before it is brought to the temple. For example, if a person bringing two loaves of bread to the high priest was stopped by a person who was not qualified to make that offer and that person demands to be given one loaf of bread, Rabbi Joshua thinks it is better to save one loaf for the temple rather than disqualifying the whole offering (based on Terumot 8:11 and 8:12).

GLEANING TIME FOR THE POOR

"Boaz and Ruth" *by Gustave Doré*

Doré Bible Illustrations · Free to Copy
www.creationism.org/images/

Ruth 2:22-23 And Naomi said unto Ruth her daughter in law, *It is good, my daughter, that thou go out with his maidens,* ... So she kept fast by the maidens of Boaz to glean unto the end of barley harvest ...

Tractate 7. Maaserot (tithes) is pronounced *mah-ah-serot.* Tithe contribution is so important to observe that it is found in several part of the Pentateuch as well as in the books of the prophets.

In modern times, the tithe can be compared to temple dues as well as to income taxes in the United States and worldwide. The commandment of the tithe was imposed on the Israelites because it was designed to support the Levite tribe, whose duty was to serve God. As it is said in the book of Deuteronomy:

> And to the House of the Levites, behold, I have given every tithe of Israel as an inheritance in exchange for their work which they perform in the tent of meeting. (Numbers 18:21)

In another book of the Pentateuch it clearly states:

> You should surely tithe all the harvest of your seed, which grows in the field, year by year. (Deuteronomy 14:2)

In the book of the prophet Malachi, we find this statement:

Bring in all the tithe to the treasury [of the temple] so there will be food in my house. (Malachi 8:9)

There are circumstances in which a person does not have to be liable to give a tithe. As it said in the Bible:

When you come into your neighbor's vineyard, you may eat grapes as you wish to your satisfaction but you may not put any [grapes] in the vessel. If you come to your neighbor's standing corn, you may pluck [corn's] ears with your hand, but you shall not move a sickle onto your neighbor's standing corn. (Deuteronomy 23:25–26)

The Mishnah concurs with the biblical instruction saying, "If a man hires a worker to help him harvest figs and the worker says, 'In condition that my son may eat instead of my receiving a salary,' then he himself may eat but if his son eats, he is liable [for paying the tithe]" (Maaserot 2:7).

The examples above clarify that there is a difference between taking goods home, in which one owes a tithe, and consuming goods in certain circumstances in which one does not have to owe a tithe.

To clarify this matter further, anything a person acquires from the field or from the herd, he must retain a tithe for the temple.

Tractate 8. Maaser sheni is also known as the second tithe (see below for pronunciation). The Talmud deducts from the Torah that there are three types of tithes (Maaserot): Tithe number one is for the Levites and is to be done every year. Tithe number two or maaser sheni—pronounced *ma-ah-ser sheh-nee*—is to be performed four times during the seven-year cycle of remission (shemitah). It is for the individual to enjoy during the pilgrimage to Jerusalem. If it is inconvenient to carry goods for a long distance, money can replace those goods. Tithe number three or maaser ani (pronounced *ma-a-ser ah-nee*) is the tithe for the poor to be distributed for all needy people in the third and the sixth year of the cycle.

To the above tithes the Torah clearly states in Deuteronomy, the following:

You shall surely tithe all the produce of your seed that comes out of the field year after year. And you shall eat before the Lord your God in the place which He will chose to have His name dwell there; the tenth of your corn, of your wine, and of your oil; and the firstlings of your herd and of your flock; so that you learn to fear the Lord your God for all the days. If the road is too far for you because you could not carry it because the place which the Lord your God will chose to have His name dwell there . . . then you shall turn[it] into money . . . and you shall use the money for whatever you wish . . . oxen or sheep or wine . . . and you shall not abandon the Levite who dwells in your gates, for he has no portion nor inheritance within you . . . At the end of every three years you shall bring forth the tenth of your increase and you shall lay it up within your gates. Then comes the Levite, because he has no portion nor inheritance, and the stranger and the orphan and the widow who are within your gates; they shall come and eat and be satisfied. (Deuteronomy 14:22–29)

Below are some observations on the maaser (tithe) as the Mishnah clarifies:

- To be considered eligible for a tithe, fruit must be ripe. When fruit or other produce are only in the budding stage, it is not ready for maaser (tithe).

- Fruit or produce found in private property is to be tithed, while food or fruit found in public road or public property do not qualify for tithing.

- Maaser sheni (the second tithe) is considered sacred, and it cannot be exchanged for another item.

- The second tithe is subject to 20 percent tax if the person bringing it to Jerusalem has only money to purchase produce and goods for the celebrations. The fifth of what he buys is taxable.

- The tithe of the poor (maaser ani) cannot be exchanged for any other tithe, and it is strictly for the needy, the widows, the fatherless children, and for those who need it the most.

- To explain this matter further, the tithe for the poor cannot be waived for any reason. It is strictly reserved for the poor and the needy.

Tractate 9. Challah or dough offering, also known as hallah, is connected to the tithe. Dough offering is a tradition that persists today. Most orthodox and conservative households buy two challahs for the Sabbath, and although we do not have a temple today, the dough offering tradition continues.

The Talmudic discussion of the hallah is based on the biblical commandment found in the book of Numbers as follows:

> The Lord spoke to Moses saying "speak to the children of Israel and tell them when you come to the land to which I bring you to then it shall be that when you eat of the bread of the land, you shall set a portion as a gift to the Lord . . . from the first of your dough, you shall set apart a contribution to the

Lord throughout your generations."
(Numbers 15:17–22)

The Mishnah says this about the mitzvah (commandment) of the hallah,

> Five kinds of grain the challah can be made of wheat, barley, spelt, oats and rye. (Hallah 1:1)

The grains may be weighed and mixed together to make the minimum quantity. The minimum quantity (to be given to the priests) is one twenty-fourth of the dough, as it is said that "the minimum measure for the hallah offering is one twenty fourth of the dough" (Hallah 2:7).

Tractate 10. Orlah—pronounced *ohr-lah*—means, in this case only, "early fruit" (before it is considered fit for consumption).

It concerns the timing in which the Israelites are permitted to enjoy the consumption of the fruit. Since various species of fruit take up to five years to ripe and become ready to eat, the Torah and the Talmud here forbid their consumption before the five-year period, with some exception cited in the Mishnah.

One important exception deals with the spot in which the trees are planted. If the trees are planted between two properties, thus serving as a fence between a private and public property, the public side was declared exempt from orlah. This means that it is not forbidden to eat fruit from the public side at any stage of the growth of the trees. The private side of the trees is subject to orlah, which means that the trees must carry ripe fruit and must be picked and consumed only during the fifth year of their growth.

Tractate 11. Bikkurim—pronounced bee-koo-reem— means the first of everything growing suitable to be brought to the temple. Bikkurim represents an important festival. It is known in today's Israel and in the Diaspora, including in the United States, as the Festival of the First Fruit. Traditionally, that festival is honored during the holiday of Shavuot, which is, most importantly, the festival of the giving of the Torah. Religious ceremonies around the world, in synagogues and temples, feature children carrying first-fruit baskets, flowers, and other items to the bimah (stage of the temple), pronounced bee-ma.

The Mishnah gives a vivid description of the ceremonies, which took place in the festivities honoring the bringing of the first fruit to the Temple. Those ceremonies were carried out from all twenty-four districts (called ma'amadot— pronounced *ma-ah-mah-dot*) of the Holy Land, as follows:

> The men of all the small towns of the Maamad assembled in the city of the Maamad, and spent the night in the town square . . . Early in the morning, the officer said, "Arise. And let us go up to Zion, to the house of the Lord our God" . . . those who lived near Jerusalem brought fresh figs and grapes, while those [coming] from a distance brought dried figs and raisins. An ox led the procession. Its horns were adorned with gold and there was an olive wreath on its head. The flute was played in front of the procession . . . The governors, chiefs and treasurers of the Temple went out to meet them . . . All the artisans of Jerusalem would rise before them and greet them: Our brothers . . .

enter in peace . . . when they reached the Temple Mount, even King Agrippa would take a basket, place it on his shoulder and walk as far as the Temple Court. When they reached the court, the Levites sang the song "I will extol you O lord, for you have raised me up and did not make my enemies rejoice over me."

The Mishnah cites two of the above quotes, which were borrowed from the book of Jeremiah (31:6) and from the book of Psalms (Psalm 30). We must note that those ceremonies took place before the destruction of the second temple, which occurred in the year 70 CE.

The biblical tradition of the priest picking up the basket from those carrying them to the Temple Mount was equally honored in the first and second temple as prescribed in Deuteronomy:

When you arrive to the land that the Lord your God is giving you as an inheritance . . . you shall take the first of every fruit in the ground . . . and place it in a basket and go to the site that the

Lord your God will chose to have His name established. And you shall come to the priest who will be present at the time . . . and the priest shall take the basket from your hand and he will place it before the altar of the Lord your God. (Deuteronomy 26:1–4)

Chapter Eight

Moed (Pronounced Moh-ed)

Second Order of the Mishnah

Introduction

Moed means "festival" or "holiday." The Israelites were instructed to observe the Sabbath and all yearly holidays. All biblical holidays commemorate the events, which happened during the exodus of the Israelites from Egypt. For example, the festival of Passover represents freedom from slavery, and Shavuot (the festival of weeks or the festival of the giving of the Torah) occurs forty-nine days after the festival of Passover. It represents two things: the giving of the Torah and the Ten Commandments from Sinai and the first harvest to be brought to the temple.

The festival of Sukkot (festival of huts) commemorates the temporary dwelling of the

Israelites in makeshift homes made of booths and bamboos for a temporary rest and dwelling in the desert. The Israelites never remained in one place for long. They kept moving and wandering for forty years until they reached the Promised Land.

Rosh Hashanah and Yom Kippur are the festivals of awe. They represent the ten days of penitence whereby every Israelite is supposed to reflect on himself or herself and concentrate on their obligation to God. The most important fast day, which is prescribed in the Torah of Moses (the Pentateuch), is Yom Kippur whereby the Israelites are supposed to fast, pray, and refrain from luxuries.

Another fast day mentioned in the scriptures but not required by the Pentateuch is the fast of Esther. Esther, the queen of Persia, ordered, through her uncle Mordecai, that the Jews of the land fast for three days and pray to God to be saved from destruction. Following a decree designed by Haman, second to the king and a Jew hater, all Jews under King Xerxes were bound for extermination. Fortunately, they survived (around 355 BCE).

The other fast days were prescribed by postbiblical scholars and are part of the Halakhah, and they are found in the Mishnah and the Shulhan Aruch. For example, the ninth day of the month of Av is a fast day, commemorating the destruction of the first and the second temple in 586 BCE and 70 CE, respectively. They were both destroyed on the same calendar day, the ninth day of the month of Av.

The Talmud discusses all the above holidays. Talmud scholars declared in their various debates how to observe those holidays. For example for Passover, they established the Seder, which is an organized, sequential ceremony included in the festival meal.

On Yom Kippur, the scholarly fathers of the Mishnah established several rituals in order to properly celebrate the fast of Yom Kippur. For example, the night before Yom Kippur, the Israelites are supposed to traditionally ask for forgiveness for their sins by sacrificing a chicken. In modern times, it is customary to contribute money for charity. The night before Yom Kippur, Rosh Hashanah, and other holidays, special prayers for that night were established since Talmudic times. Special day prayers for each holiday were established as well.

Traditionally, there are twenty-five fast days in the traditional Jewish religion. However, the frequently observed fast days number three days: Yom Kippur, Tisha Be'Av, and the fast of Esther.

Although Yom Kippur is the only day of fast prescribed by the Bible, many observing Jews additionally honor the fast of Gedaliah, the seventeenth day of Tammuz, and the fast of the firstborn (see below).

For extremely observant Jews, all fast days established by the Halakhah are observed.

The optional fast days are listed in the historical calendar. They were established to commemorate the death of various Talmudic scholars and other sad biblical events.

To summarize, the seven traditional fast days are as follows: Yom Kippur (tenth of Tishrei); the fast of Gedaliah on the third day of Tishrei (commemorating the death of Gedaliah, who was appointed by the king of Babylonia after the destruction of Jerusalem. Gedaliah was killed by fellow Israelites because he instructed the Israelites to obey the king of Babylonia); seventeenth day of Tammuz (the first temple wall was destroyed); the tenth of Tevet (Nebuchadnezzar besieged Jerusalem); the ninth of Av (remembering the destruction of the first temple and the extreme desolation of the Holy Land. Prophet Jeremiah in the book of Lamentations championed this horrible tragedy); the fourteenth of Adar (the fast of Esther); and the fast of the firstborn (commemorating the miracle in Egypt where all Egyptian firstborn boys were slain while the Jewish firstborn boys were spared). In fact, this fast is considered to be observed in sympathy to the Egyptian tragedy.

Tractate 12. Shabbat or the Sabbath day. A general observation is that the Sabbath, which falls on Saturday, is the most sacred of all holidays and sacred days. The Halakhah considers the Sabbath holier that Yom Kippur, which is the most solemn holiday of the year.

Shabbat subtractate 1–5. Fences or safeguards were established by the rabbis of the Mishnah before the Sabbath enters on Friday evening just before sundown. For example, one should not go to the barber to get a haircut or a lady should not go to the beauty salon because this might take time and interfere with the timing of the Sabbath.

One should also avoid going to a bath house or today's gym or health club on Friday evening for the same reason. A lawyer should not take a case before the Sabbath entrance.

Certain foods took a long time to cook in postbiblical times, such as meat or onions. This might not be the case today in modern times. Nevertheless, they should be ready for consumption or refrigeration by the entrance of the Sabbath.

However, the Mishnah implies that if one has started the above tasks before the Sabbath in a reasonable manner, let them finish the job and hurry home in order to observe the Sabbath.

About lighting or putting out a lamp or fire, it is well-known that one of the biblical commandments is never to light a fire on the Sabbath. However, for security reasons or for safety, if one has to put out a lamp or a fire, it will be permitted if it can save a life.

Shabbat subtractate 6: Sabbath and women. Some rules are made about how women should dress before the entrance of the Sabbath or on the day of the Sabbath. Although it is recommended that people should put on their best clothes to honor the Sabbath, we see today that observing women dress modestly in order not to attract men. Since the commandment of the mikvah (the ritual bath for women, also known as mikveh) is still observed today, the Mishnah recommends to have women avoid putting head bands or head bangles on so as to be able to completely immerse in the mikvah.

Shabbat subtractate 7: It speaks about the prohibited tasks to be done on the Sabbath day. Some light tasks are allowed, like walking to the temple, shaking hands, serving foods, and the like, but the Mishnah, unlike the Bible, has enumerated thirty-nine tasks a man should avoid on the Sabbath such as planting trees, cleaning crops, weaving, sewing, hunting, slaughtering or flaying an animal, writing, lighting or putting out a fire, carrying heavy equipment, and the like. Anything that demands effort is prohibited. One of the most prohibited tasks is lighting fire on the Sabbath.

Putting on the *tefillin*, also called phylacteries, which are worn every day in the morning prayers, are not allowed on the day of the Sabbath. Since the day of the Sabbath is so unique, there is no need to show another sign of faithfulness to God.

All observing Jews simply wear the *tallit* (also called tsisit) during the Sabbath prayer. The tallit is the garment prescribed by the Bible for the Israelites so they can remember to follow the commandments of the Torah.

Shabbat subtractate 7, 9, 13, 16, 18, and 19. These Sabbath suborders teach us the following:

- A man should not wear a military uniform on the Sabbath unless he has been wearing that uniform as part of his daily occupation. A great example is that it is normal in Israel that men and women walk around on any day, including the Sabbath, with military uniforms because military service is mandatory for most Israelis. There are exceptions to military service for men who devote their entire time to study the Torah or women who get married by the time they are called to military service.

- If a man forgot what day it was and if he were performing duties forbidden on the Sabbath, he is not considered liable. However, a person who deliberately performed duties forbidden on the Sabbath is considered liable. This problem in modern times rarely exists as almost everyone watches television or carries a cell phone and is aware of the timing of the Sabbath, especially in Israel where most public services are closed on the Sabbath.

- The Mishnah also warns us not to come close to a woman who "emits semen on the third day." This is based on the commandment found in different passages in the Pentateuch, especially written in length in Leviticus 15:19–33:

  > If a woman has a discharge of blood for many days when past her menstrual period, [then] as long as she has this discharge she is [considered] unclean just as in the days of her menstrual period. (Leviticus 15:25)

- A newborn male may be circumcised on Shabbat.

- A newborn male may be delivered on Shabbat. Midwives and doctors may be called on that day to deliver the newborn. However, the same rule does not apply to delivery of the young of cattle during the Sabbath or any religious holiday.

- A male child may be circumcised on the eighth, ninth, tenth, eleventh, and twelfth day, not before and not after. The explanation is as follows: If a child is born at the twilight time of any day of the week except Friday, this qualifies the circumcision to be done on the ninth day. If a child is born of Friday exactly during twilight, this qualifies the circumcision to be performed on the tenth day. If the child is born during a holiday that falls right after the Sabbath, the rule of circumcision is on the eleventh day. Finally, since Rosh Hashanah lasts two days, this will push the circumcision to the twelfth day after the birth of the child if the child were born at twilight on a Friday night right before Rosh Hashanah, which occurs right after Saturday.

- Normally, circumcision is done on the eighth day of the child's birth. In today's reality, as hospitals become crowded, exceptions are made, and children can be circumcised before their normal due time prescribed by the Halakhah.

- As we said before, hunting is forbidden on Shabbat. If a deer enters a house on the Sabbath and the owner shuts the door, he is considered as someone who intends to hunt, and that is forbidden. However, if another person enters the house and shuts the door without realizing there is a deer in the house, the assumed hunting is not considered a sin.

- All sacred books may be saved on Shabbat in case of fire or other calamities.

- As indicated before, an observing Jew is forbidden from lighting or putting out a fire on a Sabbath day unless a non-Jew lights or puts out the fire without direct request from the observing Jew to do so.

- The above regulations can easily be adjusted in today's modern technology of a programmed clock, which lights and puts off lights in a timely manner.

Tractate 13. Eruvin—pronounced *eh-roo-veem*—means "mixture." Eruv is the singular word for Eruvin. It involves the limited space and limited area in which observing Jews can move around and carry food or other permissible objects during a Sabbath day or a religious holiday.

Subtractate Eruvin 3, 4, 8. Since it is forbidden to move things from a private area to a public area, the history of eruv has evolved with time.

According the Bible, the Israelites were not permitted to carry any heavy item on Shabbat and holidays. They were also not permitted to leave their homes and their quarters as it said in the Bible in Exodus 36:6 and clearly in the book of Jeremiah as follows:

> Thus said the Lord; take heed to yourself and carry no burden on the Sabbath day, nor bring it to the gates of Jerusalem . . . neither do any work but hallow the Sabbath day as I commended you. (Jeremiah 17:21–22)

Some Mishnaic rabbis allowed four thousand cubits of allowed distance of movement within the eruv quarter. A cubit, as explained by Bible interpreters, is a distance from a man's elbow to the tip of the middle finger (about seventeen inches).

Other Mishnaic rabbis disagreed with that distance. In modern times, the eruv principle exists and is also a matter of controversy because the extent of its limitation is not agreed by all.

In London, Canada, the United States, and other countries, the problem of interfering with the nonreligious public exists. While religious people observe the eruv limit, nonreligious people who are their neighbors may experience inconvenience.

One way of solving this problem is the decision by local Jews to create an enclosed area where all Jewish inhabitants share food and items so they are not considered breaking the law of eruv.

By sharing a common quarter limited by a physical or symbolic wall, they share a space permitted by the Halakhah.

In conclusion of this subject of eruvin, it is permissible to carry things from one side to another, no matter how far it is, as long as it is done in an enclosed area.

The closed quarters discussed above qualify for eruv because the light work of carrying one item or another is done within an area that has set boundaries. A good modern example is the gated communities we find today everywhere in various cities. In those gated communities, the laws of eruv may not be broken among those who strictly observe the Sabbath.

Tractate 14. Pesahim is the celebration of Passover and is pronounced *peh-sah-kheem*. It is the plural of *pesah* (Passover). Pessahim is in the plural mode because there were two different celebrations of Passover: one for Judea (Jerusalem) and one for Samaria in northern Israel by the Samaritans who did not recognize Jerusalem as their only temple. They worshiped Mount Gerizim where they offered their sacrifices.

Subtractate 1–2 of Pesahim. We learn the following:

- The chametz is what is leavened and what is not kosher for Passover. It can be given to the cattle, or it can be kept separate. Some rabbis said to burn it, and others said to crumble it and throw it away.

- It must be searched the eve of Passover, traditionally, with a candle.

- The grains that are prohibited in Passover are wheat, barley, spelt, oats, and rye. However, to be kosher, they must be unleavened. The best example is the matzah. The matzah, the unleavened bread, is consumed for seven days during Israel's Passover, while, traditionally, in the Diaspora, the matzah is eaten for eight days.

Subtractate 4–8 of Pesahim. It is customary to work half a day before Passover, but one should follow the local custom (if they work more than half a day but end their work just before sundown at the eve of the holiday).

One opinion stated in this chapter is that roast meat is to be eaten as per tradition. Rabban Gamliel's view was that it was not necessary. His decision was accepted.

A newlywed woman may choose to have the Passover meal with her husband or with her father if it is her first Passover as a newlywed. Traditionally, the Passover is celebrated within the whole family.

Subtractate 9–10 of Pesahim. One cannot eat between minhah (the afternoon prayer) and the start of the Seder (the Passover ceremonious meal). After the afternoon prayer, one should restrain from eating until the evening Passover meal, thus honoring the festival and the Seder ceremony.

Rich or poor, everyone should have four cups of wine.

The *tamhui* (tamhuy) is a community food service designed for the poor or people who need immediate relief. We, in modern times, may call that the soup kitchen. It has been a tradition for thousands of years to provide matzah (matzoh) and wine for the poor in honor of Passover.

- The Passover Seder in Talmudic times was not much different than the one we celebrate in modern times. In fact, in modern times, we put equal emphasis on the way it should be celebrated by reciting the Haggadah (the recitation of the story of Passover). We even add more and more passages from modern scholars who make the story of the Exodus meaningful for the whole family, especially for the young members of the family.

- Rabban Gamliel was the initiator of the three symbols of Passover: pessah (the roasted meat invoking the old sacrifice), matzah (the unleavened bread the Israelites had to consume in the desert because they could not wait for the dough to rise as they left Egypt in a hurry), and finally, maror (the bitter herbs, which symbolize the bitter life the Israelites suffered under the Egyptians).

- The hallel (a selection of psalms praising God, which are read after the Passover meal) was also read in Mishnaic times in Passover. It is read today in the morning prayer of the pilgrimage holidays (Passover, Sukkot, and Shavuot).

Tractate 15 of Moed. Shekalim, pronounced *sheh-kah'leem* and plural of *Shekel. Shekel* was a biblical currency and is a modern currency today in Israel. This subchapter also speaks about taxes and financial obligations to the temple.

Subtractate 1–5 of Shekalim. It is about taxes. The Bible, in the book of Exodus (30:11–16), requires the amount of half a shekel to be paid from everyone, twenty years of age or older, whether the tax payer is rich or poor.

- According to the Mishnah, the tax money is due on the first of the Hebrew month of Adar, one month before the fiscal year begins on the first month of Nissan (which is the month of the celebrated Passover).

- Repairs and maintenance of the temple must be done in the month of Adar, which is one month before the Passover holiday.

- Besides the usual offering to the temple, there was the bird offering made by women after giving birth. The sin offering was accepted as well.

- The Samaritans (in the north of the Holy Land) did not have to pay taxes because they did not recognize the Temple of Jerusalem as their temple. This decision was made by Ezra the Scribe.

- There were two rooms in the temple: the Chamber of Secret Gifts (where the poor drew support from them) and the Chamber of the Vessels (where gifts were collected).

- Every thirty days, those gifts were visited by the treasurers; gifts that did not serve the temple were put aside for sale to the public.

Tractate 16 of Moed. Yoma or *the day*, pronounced *yoh-mah.* It speaks about the most solemn day of the year: Yom Kippur.

Biblical commandments in the book of Exodus, Leviticus, and Numbers emphasize the importance of that day of fast described as "a day of atonement on which expiation is made on your behalf before the Lord your God" (Leviticus 23:27–28).

The following are remarks on rituals that took place around the fast of Yom Kippur in Mishnaic times, as follows:

- Each Israelite is obligated to fast on Yom Kippur unless there is a danger to his (or her) life.

- We notice that the high priest in the first century CE was different from the high priest serving during the first temple built by King Solomon.

- The more-recent high priests mentioned in the Mishnah were not as learned as their biblical counterparts, but they were considered royalty nevertheless because they were appointed by a higher authority, such as a king or an emperor.

- It was believed that they were politically motivated because they were under the occupation of a foreign power. In this case, the Roman Empire dominated the Middle East, including the Holy Land, around the Mishnaic times.

- Ritually speaking, seven days before Yom Kippur, the high priest was assigned elders from the court. They read to him the rituals found in the book of Leviticus 16. The sacred ceremony is described as follows:

- One day before Yom Kippur, the elders presented the high priest with oxen, rams, and sheep for the ritual of Yom Kippur.

- After that, the elders of the court turned him over to the elders of the priesthood who were to administer an oath to him.

- Before the sacrifice rituals, the high priest read and was also was read passages from the scriptures in order to prepare him for the confession of the holy day.

- The confession was extremely solemn and moving as it is written in the Bible. That confession was recited while he set his hands on the bullock.

- The confession was "O God, I have committed inequities. I have transgressed and I have sinned before you . . . O God, forgive the inequities . . . I have committed and transgressed and sinned before you" (Leviticus 16:30).

- The congregation responded, "Blessed be the name of His kingdom's glory for ever and ever."

- The high priest would pronounce the unspeakable word composed of a four-letter word, which is the name of God.

- Then the high priest moved eastward, north of the altar where two he-goats were present.

One of them was to be the scapegoat and the other one for sacrifice.

- The high priest then left the he-goats and placed his hands on the bullock and made a second confession to the congregation who also answered, "Blessed be the name of His kingdom's glory for ever and ever."

- The third confession was for the house of Israel as a whole, as follows, "For on this day, He shall atone for you to cleanse you from all of your sins."

- After he pronounced the actual name of God for whom he was the only one permitted to do so, the residing priest and the standing people repeated the same blessing, glorifying God for ever and ever.

- The high priest waited for the scapegoat to reach the Judean wilderness where hills and cliffs are present. Then he began to read the appropriate biblical verses designed for Yom Kippur as written in Leviticus 16 and Leviticus 23. He then pronounced eight various blessings for the Israelites, the priests, and the Temple of Jerusalem.

- In modern times, this holy ritual of the priest blessing the congregation and the house of Israel is mentioned in the prayers for Yom Kippur. It begins on the eve of Yom Kippur. That special prayer in the beginning of the eve of Yom Kippur is called *Kol Nidrei* (which translates into "all vows").

- The contemporary way of observing Yom Kippur in the United States and in every synagogue in the world is extremely solemn and moving. In synagogues, it is the cantor of the temple who prays for the congregation and who repeats some of the words of the biblical high priest seen above.

Tractate 17: Sukkah (Booth or Hut). It speaks about the festival of Sukkot, also called the festival of tabernacles. Biblical sources of observing the festival of Sukkot (plural of *sukkah*) is found is several parts of the Bible: Leviticus 23, Exodus 23, Numbers 29, and in the books of the prophets Ezekiel, Ezra, and Nehemiah.

The following is a summary of the rules to be observed for the sukkah, according to the Mishnah and the Gemarah:

- The Sukkah must be no more than twenty *ammot* in height. One amma (singular of ammot) is a little over one foot. Rabbi Yehudah said it can have more than twenty ammot in height.

- It should not have less than ten handbreadths in height. This is another reason why the sukkah should be high enough to shelter standing people within it.

- It should be shaded and must have a roof.

- Old and new sukkot (plural of sukkah) were a subject of debate between the school of Shammai and the school of Hillel. The school of Hillel prevailed, as in many cases, because of its flexibility to the law. According to the House of Hillel, there is no time limit to how early in the year the sukkah was built for the holiday as long it was expressly built for the holiday of Sukkot.

- The sukkah can be built between trees.

- A person can be away for the holiday, without being inside the sukkah, if that person was performing a holy mission or a mitzvah (a good deed).

- Fourteen meals must be eaten inside the sukkah: two meals for each day of a seven-day celebration.

- Women, slaves, and minors are exempt from the obligation to dwell in the sukkah. Women were exempt because they were usually busy with the household and other family duties. However, they were always welcome to attend to the mitzvah of Sukkot.

- The commandment of making the blessing on the lulav and waving it during the hallel (a ritual praising God through a series of psalms) used to be done on the first day of the Sukkot. After the destruction of the second temple (70 CE), Rabbi Yohanan Ben Zakkai ruled that that ritual of the lulav be done every day of the holiday in memory of the temple.

- The lulav (a palm branch) is one of the four species used during the festival of Sukkot. The other three species are: arava (willow), hadas (myrtle), and etrog (citron). It is customary to bind two willows and three myrtles around the palm branch while holding the etrog in the left hand (for right-handed people) and while making a special blessing.

Tractate 18. Beitsah, meaning "egg," pronounced *bay-tsah,* speaks about the timing of eating an egg that has been laid on Saturday. Also this tractate lists certain things to abstain from on a holiday or a Sabbath.

Subtractate beitsah 1, 2, 5. An egg laid on the Sabbath may not be eaten the same day. It can be eaten the next day if Sunday is not a festival.

- The same rule applies to the festival of Shavuot. The sages of the Mishnah concluded that all festive foods should be prepared on nonfestive days preceding the holiday.

- If a holiday falls on a Friday before the Sabbath, the House of Hillel says one should prepare one big dish. The House of Shammai says to prepare two dishes. A dish may mean that a complete meal should be prepared ahead of the holiday.

- In modern times, all observing Jewish families prepare (cook and refrigerate) two full-service meals or more in anticipation of a holiday that falls after the Sabbath.

- The Mishnah reminds us in this tractate that a holiday that falls in the middle of the week should be considered as a Sabbath, a day of rest (see above the list of prohibited tasks on the Sabbath). Additional prohibited tasks on a holiday include climbing a tree, riding an animal, swimming, clapping hands, stomping feet, and sitting in a judgment or officiating a regular marriage or a levirate marriage.

- In modern times, dancing and stomping feet can be considered a celebration of a festival. Therefore, it is authorized even by some rabbis in a festival (see the last chapter on the *Mitnagdim* versus the *Hasidim* in regard to jubilation while praying).

- A good example of dancing celebration happens in the festival of Simhat Torah. It occurs after the festival of Sukkot. The day after the last day of Sukkot is called Shemini Atzeret (the assembly of the eighth day). It has been prescribed by the Bible. In Israel, Shemini Atzeret and Simhat Torah are celebrated simultaneously. In countries other than Israel, it is celebrated after Shemini Atzeret (as said earlier, one additional day is added for the Diaspora synagogues for pilgrimage holidays).

- That traditional day that follows the festival of Sukkot and Shemini Atzeret is a day to celebrate the spiritual treasures of Judaism: the scrolls of the Torah. Following the first part of the morning service and around the time for reading the Torah, the holy scrolls are carried multiple times by different congregants around the temple while dancing and singing takes place.

Tractate 19. Rosh Hashanah (or the New Year— literally, "the head of the year") is pronounced as it is written.

- In Jewish tradition, there are several heads of the year for several occasions. The most celebrated one is the first of the month of Tishrei, also called Rosh Hashanah, announcing the first day of the Jewish calendar and counting as the first day of the days of awe, preceding Yom Kippur, which falls on the tenth of Tishrei.

- The other popular celebrated head of the year is called Tu Bishvat. It falls on the fifteenth day of the month of Shevat. Since Mishnaic times, this day, declared by Rabbi Hillel, became the festival of trees. It is celebrated today in all Hebrew schools and Hebrew colleges, and it is also called Arbor Day. It is the time to plant new trees and to celebrate the beginning of the early spring in the Holy Land.

- Back to Rosh Hashanah, the beginning of the Jewish New Year. That timing, the first of Tishrei, which falls in autumn, was not declared by the Bible. Traditionally, the first month of the biblical year was actually in the month of Nissan, the month of the Passover celebration (when the Israelites were freed from Egypt). Rosh Hashanah has been established by the early sages to coincide with the blowing of the shofar (the ram's horn), which calls on the Israelites to take responsibility for their deeds throughout the year. The biblical source for Rosh Hashanah is found in Leviticus 23, Numbers 29, Exodus 12, Exodus 23, Exodus 34, Ezekiel 40, Psalms 81, and Nehemiah 8.

- The new moon was declared ceremoniously in ancient times. The Samaritans had their way of announcing it, even before the arrival of the month. The Mishnah declares the following people inappropriate to declare the new moon: the usurers, the gamblers, including pigeon fliers (pigeon fliers used to bet on pigeons as people bet on horses today); and the transgressors of the seventh year, meaning those who sell any produce growing in the year of remission (when the land is supposed to rest).

- The shofar used to be blown on the day of Sabbath before the destruction of the second temple. Following 70 CE, the shofar was blown only on holidays and on days of the week that do not fall on Saturday. That practice is observed to the day.

- At the conclusion of the Yom Kippur fast, we traditionally blow the shofar in the synagogues to announce the end of the fast. This practice of blowing the shofar at the end of Yom Kippur was not observed in Mishnaic times.

Tractate 20. Taanit, meaning "fast days," is pronounced *tah-ah-neet*. Although this subject could have been under a previous tractate about Yom Kippur (Yoma), the Mishnah connected fast days to prayer for rain. It was normal to pray for rain in times of drought or when the rain did not fall during the proper season.

- Several legends are written around prayers for rain. The most popular one was the one about Honi the Circle Maker who drew a circle around him and vowed not to leave that circle until it began to rain. When the rain came down lightly, he was told to pray for some more rain. When the rain was overwhelming, he was told to pray again until the rain came down normally.

- Rabbi Judah said it was best to pray for rain during the Passover holiday, and Rabbi Meir reinforced his view by saying it was best to keep praying until the end of the month of Nissan (meaning to keep praying for another week after the holiday until the end of the month).

- It is also reported that the mishnaic worshipers used to pray for rain in the month of Heshvan (the second month of the calendar year). When the rain did not fall, they fasted three days and then seven days when it still did not rain. During those fast days, they blew the shofar and they closed their shops.

- It is also reported that the two happiest days of the year were the fifteenth day of Av (six days after Tisha Be'Av) and Yom Kippur, when the daughters of Jerusalem went out dancing in the vineyards.

- That custom had disappeared as the most solemn day of the year remains Yom Kippur, and there is no celebration or food involved during that day.

Tractate 21. Megillah, meaning "scroll," is pronounced *meh-gee-lah*.

- Although there are five books in the Bible to qualify to be a megillah (scroll), this tractate speaks about the book of Esther. The five scrolls spoken about earlier are the books of Esther, Lamentations, the Song of Songs, Ecclesiastics, and the book of Ruth.

- In contemporary times, the megillah of Esther is read on the eve of the Purim festival, which falls on the fifteenth day of Adar. The megillah is also read in the morning prayer of *Hag Purim* (the festival of Purim).

- The Mishnah tells us that the megillah can be read on the eleventh, twelfth, thirteenth, fourteenth, and fifteenth of Adar, but not before and not after those days.

- The Mishnah reminds us that a transgression committed on a Jewish holiday or a Sabbath can be punishable by the court. However, a transgression committed on Yom Kippur, the most solemn day of the Jewish year, is handled by God Himself.

- The megillah may be read while standing or sitting.

- On Mondays and Thursdays, three people may be called to read or to be read to a portion of the Torah of the week. This is called an *alyah* (plural *alyot)*, meaning, literally, "ascending to read the Torah" or "the calling to the Torah."

- An alyah, while a portion of the Torah is read, must have at least three verses. A minor may read the Torah, but he cannot make the adult blessings before reading the Torah.

- Important prayers like the Shema (Hear, O Israel) cannot take place in a congregation without the quorum of ten people. The same applies to the blessing of the *cohen* (a member of the congregation descending from the house of the Levites, who were the biblical priests). The Holy Ark cannot be opened without the said quorum.

- A blind man may recite the blessing of the Shema.

Tractate 22. Moed Katan or small holiday is pronounced *moh-ed-katan*. It falls between the first and the last day of a long holiday containing seven or eight days. Seven days are observed in the Holy Land. However, out of Israel, another day is added, fulfilling the postbiblical tradition observed in Talmudic times when there was no way of knowing exactly when the festival began. The exact timing of the holiday anywhere in the world is well-known today, thanks to modern and rapid communications, but the tradition continues even to the twenty-first century.

The following rules and remarks were established by the Talmudic rabbis for the Moed Katan:

- Do not mix a joy with a joy. Meaning, no celebrations are to be made during a joyous holiday. There is no need to have another celebration like marriage, but a divorced man can remarry his previous wife.

- Women can put on jewelry or use other means to look well for the midholiday.

- Anything that has to do with legal matters during the midholiday is allowed. The legal things allowed are letters of divorce, deeds, wills, arbitrators, and similar court matters.

However, new marriage contracts and celebrations are not allowed.

Tractate 23. Hagigah is a celebration involving sacrifice and is pronounced *hah-gee-gah*.

- Since the sacrifice involves a long march for pilgrimage to Jerusalem, physically and mentally challenged people are not allowed to participate in it. In modern times, that practice does not exist, but physically limited people are allowed to perform any religious obligation as long as they are able to do so.

- Women are exempt of hagigah because they are busy taking care of household chores.

- The midholiday was carefully observed in Mishnaic times, and it is still honored in our days in all synagogues worldwide.

DISCUSSING THE INGREDIENTS
THE SABBATH CANDLE SHOULD
BE COMPOSED OF

מסורת
הש"ס

במה מדליקין פרק שני שבת

עין משפט
נר מצוה

Chapter Nine

Nashim (On Women)

Third Order of the Mishnah

The order of Nashim (pronounced *nah-sheem*) discusses and debates the laws of marriage and divorce and the right of women in civil matters.

That order consists of seven tractates. The order begins with tractate 24.

- *Tractate 24.* Yevamot, pronounced *yeh-vah-mot*—talks about levirate marriage. It is the obligation of the surviving brother to marry the wife of his deceased brother. The intention is to preserve the generation of the family. Various thoughts are brought by the scholars on this matter, but most of them follow the instruction commanded by the Torah as it is detailed in Deuteronomy.

"If brothers live together and one of them dies without a son, the wife of the deceased shall not marry a stranger, outside her milieu. Her husband's brother shall come to her and marry her as per the levirate [law]" (Deuteronomy 25:5).

Marriage certificate according to the Moses tradition

קול חתן וקול כלה

Certificate of Marriage

This is to Certify

hat on the ___3ʳᵈ___ day of the
veek, the ___1ˢᵗ___ day of the
nonth of ___Teus___ in the
year 572_, corresponding to the
___1ˢᵗ___ day of ___January___ 19

he holy Covenant of Marriage

vas entered into at ___Cakeville Ind.___
between the Bridegroom
_____
and his bride
_____

e said Bridegroom made the
g declaration to his Bride:

thou my wife according to the law
and Israel. I faithfully promise that
 true husband unto thee; I will honor
ish thee; I will work for thee; I will
 nd support thee, and will provide all
 cessary for thy sustenance, as
 it beseemeth a Jewish husband to
 so take upon myself all such
obligations for thy maintenance,
rescribed by our religious statute"

 the said Bride has plighted her troth
, in affection and in sincerity, and has
n upon herself the fulfillment of all
es incumbent upon a Jewish wife.

is Covenant of Marriage was duly
s and witnessed this day according
sage of Israel.

בשבת _____
שנת חמשת אלפים ושבע מאות
_____ לבריאת עולם, למנין שאנו מונין
_____ במדינת אמריקא הצפונית
ב״ר _____
הדא בתולתא _____
הוי לי לאנתו
ה וישראל ואנא אפלח ואוקיר ואיזון ואפרנס
כי כהלכות גוברין יהודאין דפלחין ומוקירין וזנין
ין לנשיהון בקושטא ויהיבנא ליכי מהר בתוליכי
די מאתן דחזי ליכי מדאוריתא ומזוניכי
בי וסיפוקיכי ומיעל לותיכי כאורח כל ארעא
מרת _____ בתולתא דא
ה לאנתו, ודין נדוניא דהנעלרת ליה מבי
בין בכסף בין בזהב ובין בתכשיטין
דלבושא בשמושי דירה, ובשמושי דערסא הכל קבל
_____ חתן דנן במאה זקוקים
וצב _____
להון דיליה עוד מאה זקוקים כסף צרוף אחרים
סך הכל מאתים זקוקים כסף צרוף וכך אמר
_____ חתן דנן אחריות
נבתא דא נדוניא דין ותוספתא דא קבלית עלי ועל יׄת
להתפרע מן כל שפר ארג נכסין וקנינין דאית לי
כל שמיא, דקנאי ודעתיד אנא למקנא,
דאית לדהון אחריות ודלית להון אחריות
יהון אחראין וערבאין לפרוע מנהון שטר
א דא נדוניא דין ותוספתא דא מנאי ואפילו
מא דעל כתפאי בחיי ובתר חיי מן יומא דנן ולעלם.
ת שטר כתובתא דא נדוניא דין ותוספתא דא
_____ חתן דנן
כל שטרי כתובות ותוספתות דנהגין בבנות
העשויין כתקון חכמינו זכרונם לברכה
אסמכתא ודלא כטופסי דשטרי וקנינא
_____ חתן דנן
בתולתא דא
מה דכתוב ומפורש לעיל במנא דכשר
א ביה והכל שריר וקים.

- *Tractate 25.* Ketubot or marriage agreement is pronounced as *keh-too-bot*. It is, in short, a prenuptial agreement between the intended wife and the intended husband. It is a marriage contract preceding the marriage itself. The Bible and the Talmud give ample rights to the woman as she deserves respect before and after marriage.

- *Tractate 26.* Nedarim (vows) is pronounced as *ne-dah-reem*. According to the Bible, a husband can cancel the vow of a woman. At the same time, a father can cancel the vow of a daughter. If the husband or the father ignore the woman's pledge, then the vow stands, and the pledge of the woman is honored.

- *Tractate 27.* Nazir. A nazir is an ascetic. An ascetic dedicates himself to God in abstaining from cutting hair, drinking wine, and touching a dead corpse. It is not compulsory on anyone to be a nazir except for those who want to serve God and want to be introduced to the priesthood. Samson, for example, was a nazir but not a priest. His strength was in his abstinence in drinking wine, not cutting his hair, and resisting women. When he gave in to Delilah by cutting his hair and drinking wine, his strength left him. His strength came back when his hair grew again after he prayed to God.

- Samuel, on the other hand, was closely supervised by his mother, Hannah, to become a nazirite. An indispensable prophet, judge, and priest, he largely contributed to bringing the Israelites back to God with his words of wisdom. Although the Bible reports that the only thing Samuel observed was growing his hair, he was considered a nazir (nazirite) by some Talmud scholars and non-nazirite by other rabbis.

- This tractate also speaks about the fact that a woman can also become a nazirite, but her vow can be dismissed or canceled by her husband or father. However, a woman can go through it if no one in her family interferes in her vow.

- *Tractate 28. Sotah* is pronounced *so-tah*. It literally means "deviating." This tractate deals with a married woman who is unfaithful to her husband. She could deny her accusers. However, if she were found unfaithful, she was brought to the priest and was given "bitter waters" to drink. According to the Bible, the drinking of bitter water could show and prove if she was indeed a sotah (deviant). If her drinking the waters resulted in her death, it proved that she was unfaithful, and therefore, she was punished for her sin.

- Some modern rabbis wonder about this rule of making a woman drink bitter waters. Nevertheless they accept it as a *hok*, which is an unexplained rule of law. After the 70 CE, that rule has been modified by Rabbi Yohanan Ben Zakkai.

- *Tractate 29.* Gittin is the plural of get (bill of divorce). It is pronounced *geet-tin*. This tractate discusses divorce between a man and a woman. In this case, if a man finds something extremely wrong in a woman, he is entitled to divorce her by according her the bill of divorce, which is called a get. The Talmudic rabbis discussed the following quote from the Bible about that divorce,

When a man takes a wife and is intimate with her, and it happens that she does not find favor in his eyes because he discovers in her an immoral matter, and he writes for her a bill of divorce and places it into her hand, and sends her from his house. And she leaves his house and goes and marries another man. If the other man despises her and writes her a bill of divorce, and places it into her hand and sends her from his house, or if the latter man who took her as a wife dies, [then] the first husband who sent her out cannot take her back to be his wife after she became impure. (Deuteronomy 24:1–4)

- *Tractate 30.* Kidushim, pronounced *kee-doo-sheem*, means "sanctification." The sanctification takes place between a man and a woman. The Gemarah states that a women can be married or, in the words of the Mishnah, can belong to a man through three things: money, deed, and intercourse.

- The explanation of the Mishnah is as follows: Money is given to the woman or her family from the intended groom in order to assure the family of his good intentions to marry. The other way of marrying is through a deed or a contract of marriage, stating the holiness of the union, and before witnesses, it becomes a valid marriage. The third way is when two people are involved intimately and have all the intention to be with each other forever and create or continue a family. This is accepted in the case of a levirate marriage (as seen before).

Concluding this portion of Nashim, a widow can marry her brother-in-law as per the biblical commandment of *ybbum* (levirate marriage). Finally, a woman acquires her freedom through her husband's death and is free to remarry.

This was true in ancient times as it is true today.

In modern times, a ring is given to the bride as a token of eternal love. In some countries today, money and goods are still given to the bride's family before a wedding is performed as it was done in ancient times.

KETUBBAH—AN ALL ARAMAIC
TRADITIONAL CERTIFICATE OF MARRIAGE

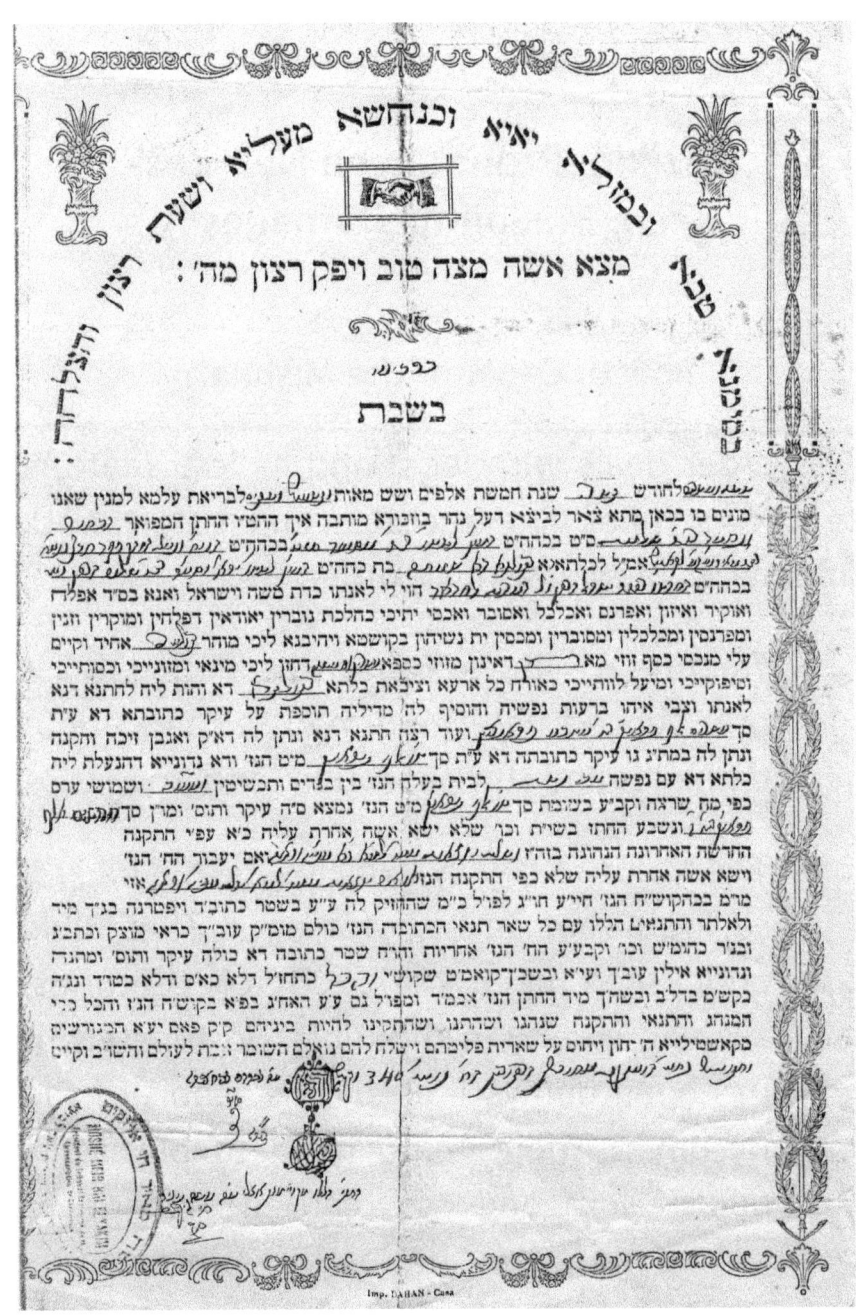

Chapter Ten

Nezikin (Pronounced *Neh-Zee-Keen*, Meaning "Damages")

Fourth Order of the Mishnah

This order deals with legal and judicial matters as follows: it has nine tractates, and it starts with tractate 31 of the Mishnaic order.

- *Tractate 31.* Bava Kama (the first gate) is pronounced *bah-va-ka-mah*. It talks about damages and compensation for damages.

- The Mishnah clearly explains the old biblical saying about an "eye for eye." That Bible quote had been criticized for centuries, alleging cruelty in the Bible. Fortunately, it has been demystified by the rabbis of the Mishnah. There is no need to physically punish someone who caused damage to someone's eyes. The matter is resolved by the court leaders who determine the fine and the compensation for damages.

- If an ox charges another ox and hits a woman and she miscarries, no damages are paid for the embryo. But if a man hits another man and, consequently, hits a woman and she miscarries, then the court decides the fine for the damages to the woman. The court has differentiated between the above damages caused to a woman and, obviously, could not hold the owner of the ox responsible.

- In case of death of a victim of an injury, compensation remains in order. The court compensates the heirs of the family of the victim.

- The following factors are considered when a man injures another man: as in modern times, the liability included pain, healing, loss of time, and indignity.

- Although the term *indignity* is not a popular word in the modern insurance vocabulary, the equivalent of that is what we might call today *pain* and *suffering*.

- This is comparable to today's compensation in case of, for example, an auto accident: the guilty driver's insurance compensates the victim or victims for damages to bodily injury and hospitalization as well as for loss of wages while the victim is recovering.

- The Mishnah expounds on this matter in case the injury to the victim still causes pain after it was already settled. However, once the victim is completely healed, the case is closed.

- Compensation for injury applies to a blind man or a sleeping man when injured. This is obvious, and the law of the Mishnah is not different from today's law.

- When a man falls from a roof and injures someone, he is liable for damages but not for indignity as the Mishnah puts it. The reason being is that the man had no intention of hurting or degrading someone by falling from the roof.

- When someone had his books or articles stolen and the thief was identified, the court demands full recovery of the articles. This is different from today's law, which requires, besides full recovery, a penalty for theft.

- The Mishnah says further that if the owner of the lost articles does not report the theft, the stolen things cannot be recovered.

Tractate 32. Bava Metziah (the middle gate or the middle part) is pronounced *bah-va-metsi-ah* and deals with property laws and torts.

- Unlike in modern times where we swear in court to tell the truth and nothing but the truth, even if the truth is perceived differently by the accused and the accuser, the oath in Talmudic times was the ultimate basis for the court to make a judgment.

- In this part, the Mishnah speaks about two people who found an item in public property. Each person claims it is his. In this case, the item or the value should be divided between them if they both swear that they own no less than half of the item.

- Furthermore, any fraction of the property claimed by both men is awarded by the court following their swearing. We see here how taking an oath is taken seriously by the deciding court.

- In another case, if a man is looking for his lost item and his father's item simultaneously, the Mishnah says that the son's property takes precedence. If the son were looking for his teacher's property while looking for his father's property, the Mishnah says his teacher's property takes precedence. However, if his father were a sage or a scholar, then his father's property takes precedence over his teacher's.

- That law may not be accepted in our time.

- Two people deposit money with a third person. One person deposited double of what the other deposited. When it is time to withdraw that money, both men claim the larger amount deposited by one of them. In this case, the court decides that both men get each the smaller amount and that the rest of the money is to remain in escrow.

- Merchants should be careful not to defraud customers by offering two or more products while the cheaper product is presented to the client as the more expensive.

- A merchant may lower the price of his merchandise. After debate between the sages, this decision remained without change.

- The sages also debated whether it was legal for the merchants to give small gifts to children so they would keep coming back (in this case, it was parched corn or nuts). Although some rabbis objected because of business fairness, the decision remained as such, meaning that it was permissible for the merchant to offer small snacks to the children so they would come back and, naturally, bring their parents with them.

- In comparing this ancient decision to today's way of life, it is perfectly normal for merchants to offer small gifts or snacks to children or adults in order to earn their business.

- A shopkeeper working for someone else must receive a salary and should not work on a contingency basis. The Mishnah calls it half a profit. The same principle applies when a person gives another person chicken or calves and expects a profit from those chicken and calves without giving a salary to the grower. The Mishnah says that the worker must be paid for his work unless the owner agrees with the grower to have a fifty-fifty profit agreement on condition that the calves are at least a third grown.

- Prices of goods and produce should not be fixed until the market price is known. The market price is determined only after the crop is ready and all growing expenses have been taken into consideration. They should not be determined arbitrarily by any producer until all produce is available for marketing throughout the land.

- Money should not be loaned to borrowers at interest as it is prescribed in several parts of the Torah.

- Before a field is rented or leased, it is important to determine if the field has a potential to be fertile with irrigation means. If the field dries out and if it gives poor crops or no crops, then the leaser must pay the agreed-on price. But if he were told ahead of time that this field is irrigated and it has an orchard, therefore, the price of the lease should be adjusted, even as, in this case, the agreement is to be paying the lease through the crops of the field.

- Similarly, if a man leases a field from another man for ten units of wheat and the wheat turned out poor, the leaser must pay the agreed-on price. However, if the crop turned out well, the leaser cannot switch the good grain for a poorer grain in order to pay the lease.

Tractate 33. Bava Batra (the last gate) is pronounced *bah-va-batra.* It is is the third part that talks about property rights and business relationships. It deals with land and land ownership between people.

- If a man builds a fence on three sides of a surrounding field, the neighbor with the open side is not obligated to participate in the cost of the three built fences. However, if that man takes advantage of the situation and builds the last fence to complete the closure of the field, the court says that he is liable to pay for his fence and, furthermore, for half of the expenses for the already-established three neighboring fences.

- The sages of the court in the Mishnah decided that all tenants of a courtyard situated away from a public road should share the cost for a gatehouse and a door of the said courtyard.

- City taxes were paid then as they are paid nowadays. A person has to reside in the city for twelve months in order to qualify as a taxpayer. However, if the person bought a house before the year was up, that person is automatically liable to pay taxes.

- In protecting people's privacy, the court ruled that "no one may open a bakery or a dyer's shop under another man's warehouse, nor may he maintain a cow barn nearby" (Bava Batra 2:3). The law obviously protects the neighbors from excessive noise, offensive odors, and harmful smoke.

- No one can open a shop in a courtyard because he could get complaints about too much traffic and noise in a residential area. However, a man can make articles inside the courtyard, and he can sell them outside the courtyard, in an open market.

- When one sells a ship or a wagon or a yoke, there must be an understanding about whether other articles or furniture are included in the sale's agreement. For example, a sale of a wagon drawn by mules and a yoke worn by oxen should be determined beforehand between the buyer and the seller.

- This is obvious as the laws of today strive to list all the details of the sale before it is signed by the parties.

- Scales must be cleaned every thirty days by a wholesaler, but for a small producer-seller, once every twelve months is sufficient. This is to prevent fraud as it is written in several parts of the Torah and approved by the scholars of the Mishnah.

- In modern times, scales and other machines designed to serve goods or services are periodically calibrated.

- The Mishnah here makes a final remark in Bava Batra about the biblical daughters of Zelofehad who were mentioned in the Torah as they succeeded to inherit their father's property.

- Before that, women were not entitled to inheritance. What is more, the Mishnah added that they inherited a double portion because their father, Zelofehad, was a firstborn. The Torah speaks about this in the book of Numbers. As a result of the daughters of Zelophehad's protest and request, a new law was created by God and communicated to Moses, thus giving to the surviving daughters the land and holding of the missing father. This law was valid only if no son was left in the family. But if there were no son or daughter left in the family, justice was made by leaving the property to the closest relative alive. As is it said in the book of Numbers:

> They stood before Moses and before Eleazar the priest and before the chiefs and the whole assembly, at the entrance of the Tent of Meeting, saying, "Our

father died in the wilderness. He was not among the community which gathered against God within the Korah community. For he died from his own sin, and he did not have any sons. Why should the name of our father be done away with from his family because he has no son? Give us, I pray, a possession among the brothers of my father." And Moses brought the matter before the Lord. And the Lord said to Moses, "The daughters of Zelophehad speak right. Indeed you shall give them a hereditary holding among their father's kinsmen; pass their father's estate to them." (Numbers 27:2–5)

- "If there are no brothers to his father you shall assign his property to his nearest relative, in his own family and he shall inherit it. This shall be a statute of judgment to the children of Israel as the Lord has commanded Moses" (Numbers 27:1–7).\

DEALING WITH THE TIMING
TO RECITE THE SHEMA

מאימתי · פרק ראשון · ברכות ב

מאימתי

Braahot T.   1   אלף   [ברכות]

130

Tractate 34. Sanhedrin or the high court. It is pronounced *san-hed-reen*. It talks about criminal cases. It also compares noncapital punishment to capital punishment, including the death penalty.

- This Sanhedrin tractate can be considered the most important tractate of the Mishnah when it comes to legal matters and capital punishments.

- It is important to know in this tractate that the number of members for the Sanhedrin and all the laws for capital and noncapital punishment were based on what the Torah or the Pentateuch said in different parts of the Bible.

- For example, the number of the Sanhedrin members should be seventy-one (71). The Mishnash first quotes God saying to Moses to gather seventy men of the elders of Israel (Numbers 11:16). Since Moses was the leader of the elders, he was assumed to be the seventy-first member of the judging body.

- There was also the small Sanhedrin, which did not deal with capital punishment, and it was justified by the rabbis to amount to twenty-three judges by quoting various parts of the Torah and coming up with that number.

- Unrelated to the subject of Sanhedrin, the Mishnah says in this tractate that it was agreed that ten people are enough to make an assembly with the minimum amount of ten people. This is what is called a quorum (minyan) in order to conduct a full service. A service can take place without a quorum, but certain parts of the prayer cannot be recited without the minimum quorum of ten.

- The Sanhedrin has ample authority, which might be compared to the Senate and House of Representatives of some states in the Western democracies, particularly the United States. For example, the Sanhedrin can declare war, which, in this case, could be called voluntary war:

> A high Priest can be tried only by a court of seventy-one. A voluntary war can be decreed only by a court of seventy-one. Additions to the city of Jerusalem can be

sanctioned only by a court of seventy-one. Sanhedrins for the tribes can be authorized only by a court of seventy-one. A city can be declared an apostate city . . . only by decision of a court of seventy-one. (Sanhedrin 1:5)

- Any contemporary lawyers or judges may be impressed with the depth of some of the rules while an investigation is taking place for capital and noncapital punishment written in the Mishnah, notably in Sanhedrin 4:1, as follows:

The form of investigation is the same in non-capital cases, as it written [in the Torah, Leviticus 24:22] . . . Non-capital suits are decided by three and capital cases by twenty-three judges . . . in non-capital cases, a verdict may be reversed from conviction to acquittal, or from acquittal to conviction; capital cases may be decided by a majority of one for acquittal, but for conviction, only by a majority of two. In non-capital cases, a verdict may be reversed from conviction to acquittal, or from acquittal to conviction. But in capital cases, a verdict can only be reversed from conviction to acquittal. In non-capital cases, everyone may argue for or against the defendant; in capital cases, everyone may argue for acquittal but not for conviction . . . non-capital suits are tried by day and concluded at night . . . capital suits must be tried by day and concluded by day . . . no trial may be held on Friday or on the eve of a festival. (Sanhedrin 4:1)

- The court has a special address for witnesses to capital punishment before they come to court to testify, as follows:

In non-capital cases a man can make monetary restitution and be forgiven, but in capital cases his blood and the blood of his descendants, to the end of time

are the witness's responsibility . . .
Whosoever preserves a single soul
in Israel is given merit by Scripture
as though he had saved an entire
world. (Sanhedrin 4:5)

- Although four forms of death were available to the court (stoning, burning, death by the sword, and strangulation), the Mishnaic process of conducting a capital crime did not seem to arrive at performing the abovementioned forms of death for the defendants of a crime. The rules for death penalty seemed to be theoretical, especially after the Roman Empire took over the Middle East, including the Holy Land. Therefore, in Mishnaic times, the death penalty discussed by the rabbis was to be avoided and kept only as a very last resort. Also, the Mishnah states that even convicted criminals have a place in the world to come.

- The final portion of this tractate deals with two more concepts:

1. The first is about a rebellious child and his punishment. The Gemarah (Gemara) reports

that there has never been a stubborn and rebellious child as reported in the Bible (Deuteronomy 21).

2. The second concept reported in this final part of the Sanhedrin is the eternity of the Israelite people as it is written in the beginning of Pirkey Avot and the book of Isaiah,

> All Israelites will have a share in the world to come. They shall inherit the land forever…[except] anyone who says that the Torah was not divinely revealed; and an apikoros [epicurean] . . . also anyone who pronounces the Divine Name as it is spelled. (Sanhedrin 8:5 and Sanhedrin 10:1)

- An apikoros was that Israelite who was inspired by the Epicurean philosophy, which penetrated the Holy Land during its occupation by foreign powers. The apikoros did not accept the Halakhah and the Torah as the only way to believe in the God of the Israelites.

Tractate 35. Makkot (hits or lashes) is pronounced *mah-kkot*. It deals with banishment for a murder caused by accident. It also deals with lashes as punishment.

- When lashes are administered, they shall be no more than thirty-nine because at forty lashes, the guilty person is degraded.

- It also talks about the cities of refuge. No guilty man with blood on his hands can take refuge in those cities. The people admitted in the city of refuge are the people who unwittingly committed a murder or caused a loss of life by accident.

- The Mishnah reports the following:

  This is the general rule: when death is caused by a downward movement [for example, a man descending a ladder, falls and kills another person], banishment occurs. But if the death is caused not a result of a downward movement, [an example of a man mounting a ladder, accidentally falls and kills someone] there is no banishment. (Makot 2:1)

- The Mishnah concurs with the biblical rules of banishment and nonbanishment to refuge cities, as written in Numbers 35. It also concurs with the location of the cities mentioned in the same chapter in the book of numbers (chapter 35).

- Six cities of refuge are located as follows: three cities in the east side of the Jordan River and the other three cities inside the Holy Land. In biblical terms, the Holy Land was named Canaan (Numbers 35:14).

Tractate 36. Shevuot (oaths and pledges) is pronounced *she-voo-ot*. It deals with oaths as prescribed by the Bible. Every pledge must be fulfilled, and every man must stand behind his oath.

- There are different kinds of oaths. There is a *vain oath*. For example, if someone swears that he saw a flying camel or that he saw a snake as thick as large tree trunk, this is a vain oath, and it carries no weight. If a man swears to annul a mitzvah(a religious commandment or a religious good deed) and it is willful, it carries liability, and it deserves flogging. However, if it is done unwittingly, there is no punishment involved.

- An example of an *oath of testimony* is an oath by which a person adjures two other people to testify after they previously said that they did not have any testimony. The Mishnah finds them liable.

- The third oath mentioned in the tractate of Shevuot is for those people who are exempt from paying. A few examples can be those who have been robbed, workers who did not get paid, people who have been injured, and shopkeepers who claim that they have already paid their suppliers when the suppliers claim a settlement. Since swearing in court is extremely serious, the testimony of those who have been victimized can support their claims by their swearing in front of a judge.

Tractate 37. Eduyot (testimonies) is pronounced *eh-doo-yot*. After the destruction of the second temple (70 CE) and the removal of Rabban Gamliel II, it was necessary for the remaining scholars and judges to consider the majority rule to decide a case. Here, we also find differences of opinion between the House of Hillel and the House of Shammai. Since those houses were the most respected in their opinions, their decision was not always accepted by a majority, even as their opinions were considered the wisest. Consequently, legal matters were decided by a majority body.

Tractate 38. Avodah Zara (pronounced as written) is idolatry or a foreign way of worshiping. It deals with foreign worship and the interaction between Jews and non-Jews. Three days before a non-Jewish festival, it is forbidden to borrow or loan to a heathen any money. It is even forbidden to receive money from them. One scholar disagrees (Rabbi Yehuda). He says that it is permitted to receive money for something promised even in those three days before the festival of non-Jews.

- The Israelite population in the Holy Land and in the Diaspora led to constant spiritual battles against idol-worshiping. In the Torah, we find multiple warnings about foreign worship. The most recited warning is included in the daily prayer Shemah Israel (Hear, O

Israel). Nevertheless, many biblical Israelites and Jews in the Diaspora succumbed to those foreign temptations.

- This tractate establishes a safeguard or a fence by commanding all observing Jewish men and women to stay away from idol worshippers. For example, a woman or a man should not be alone with an idol worshipper, and cattle should not be kept in the barns of heathen-owned inns. An Israelite woman should not act as a midwife to a heathen woman.

- It is noteworthy that the Talmudic sages never considered Christians and Moslems idol worshippers because they were monotheists, as in the Jewish religion. In some cases, through two thousand years, Christians blamed Jews for being wrongly taken for idol worshippers. It took a long time to pacify and rectify the word *pagan* or *heathen* found in the Talmud and the Mishnah (see chapter 18).

Avot (forefathers) or Ethics of the Fathers is an extremely interesting chapter in itself. It is included in this Order. However, because of its intensity, we shall have a detailed analysis in chapters 13, 14, and 15 of this book. It is considered one of the sixty-three tractates of the Mishnah.

Tractate 39. Horayot (decisions) is pronounced *ho-rah-yot.* It deals with three different decisions of the high priest. The first decision is for the high priest making expiation for the people who committed an act unwittingly. The second case is about a priest himself making a decision in error. In the first case, we find the answer in the book of Numbers chapter 15:22–31. The second case is discussed in Leviticus 4:22.

In both cases, the high priest and the people offer specific sacrifices for specific sins. The third case concerns a bad decision from a high priest. In that case, the Bible and the Halakhah find that the high priest who deliberately made a bad decision is considered lower than the lowest people in the congregation.

In summarizing this chapter on damages, we can see how many ancient laws are similar to the laws of today.

Chapter Eleven

Kodashim (Pronounced *Ko-Dah-Sheem*) or Sacred Matters

Fifth Order of the Mishnah

This order deals with sacrifices, purity, impurity, and other transgressions and how to correct them.

The Bible prescribes a variety of sacrifices and offerings to the temple for different occasions. There are daily sacrifices, sacrifices for sins committed against God, sins committed deliberately or inadvertently. The following are the various sacrifices commented on by the Mishnah:

Tractate 40. Zevahim (sacrifices) is pronounced *zeh-vah-heem*. It speaks about sacrifices, as follows:

- **Olah** (burnt offering). Olah means "mounting" (as in mounting smoke when an animal is completely burned). It is offered daily, on Sabbath, and on Yom Kippur.

- **Hattat** (sin offering). It originates from the word *het* (sin). It is an offering for an unwittingly committed sin. (It is largely stated in Leviticus 4 and Leviticus 5.)

- **Asham** (guilt offering). It is done after a restitution has been made to the victim of an accidental offense.

- **Shelamin** (peace offering). It derives from the words *shalom* (peace) and *shalem* (complete). It is a peace offering for various occasions. Some of them are obligatory, and some of them are optional.

- **Bechor** (firstborn). As stated in the Pentateuch, the first issue of the womb belongs to God, whether it is human or animal. As it said, "You shall surely redeem the first born of a man and you shall redeem the first born of an impure animal" (Numbers 18:15).

- **Maaser Behemah** (the tithe of an animal). This is pronounced *mah-ah-ser*. The tithe of an animal should be given to the temple. We find this precept in the last two sentences of the book of Leviticus, saying, "And every tithe of the herd and flock and all that passes under the shepherd's staff, the tenth [animal] will be holy to the Lord. He [the giver] should not discern between good and bad [animal] and he should not substitute it...." (Leviticus 27: 32–33).

- this subject is also discussed in tractate 45, below.

Notes on Zevahim

Sacrifices that were made in the desert ceased when the Israelites entered the Holy Land. They were performed by the priests and only in Jerusalem.

From the Mishnah we learn that

"When they came to Jerusalem, individual altars were forbidden and never again permitted . . . the most sanctified sacrifices were consumed inside the curtains, while the second sacrifices were eaten . . . within the walls of Jerusalem" (Zevahim 14:8).

Tractate 41. Menahot (flour offerings) is pronounced *me-nah-hot* (plural of *minhah*). This was popular with poor people who could not afford to offer cattle or sheep to the high priest. Meal offerings were acceptable as well.

- There is no definite rule on how valuable the gift or sacrifice should be. It is commensurate with the financial means of the person offering. A meal offering of flour is acceptable on condition that it will be supplemented with oil and frankincense.

- "When anyone brings a meal offering to the Lord, his offering shall be of fine flour, and he shall pour oil on it and put frankincense upon it" (Leviticus 2:1).

Tractate 42. Hullin (profane matters) is pronounced *hoo-leen*. It deals with laws of dietary nature, such as the prohibition of mixing meat and milk for consumption as it is said in the Torah (Deuteronomy 14:21), "Do not boil a kid in its mother's milk."

- However, fish and milk can be boiled together. According to Hullin 8:1, the House of Hillel and the House of Shammai disagreed about exposing meat and milk products on the same table. The House of Shammai, who was always strict, did not forbid that. The House of Hillel, however, forbade exposing on the same table meat and milk. That was unusual because, normally, the House of Hillel was almost always flexible.

- Another Talmudic discussion about the mixing of meat and milk came up between the rabbis regarding fowl. Although the Torah did not specifically mention fowl to be in the same category as a cow or a sheep, the rabbis, since Ezra the Scribe, forbade the mixing of fowl with milk. Since chicken meat looks somewhat like cattle meat, they forbade the boiling of chicken and other fowl in milk, thus creating a cautious fence around the commandment of the Torah.

- Suborder Hullin also speaks about sending the mother bird away when one finds a nest. The Bible forbids the taking of the eggs and the hatchlings in the presence of the mother bird. Literally, it says that you should send the mother away, and then you can take the baby birds to yourself. Basically, it is not intended to disrupt the life of a mother bird and its nest. The intention is, if you really have to

147

choose between taking the mother bird or the baby birds, then you can take the baby birds, but you must let the mother bird go.

- To be clear, it is not a commandment to take the birds away from their mother. Some people might want to do that. In our time, we have the tendency to leave the mother and its birds alone.

Tractate 43. Bechorot (firstborn) is pronounced *beh-kho-rot*. According to the Torah, every firstborn male Israelite is dedicated to God. This means that he belongs to God and he must be redeemed by his parents. The ceremony of redeeming the firstborn Israelite is called *pidyon habben* (redemption of the child). The same thing applies to kosher animals such as a bull or a goat. They belong to God, and they must be redeemed by their owner.

- A Talmudic discussion among Mishnaic rabbis on this order of Zevahim goes like this: It is about a woman who had a miscarriage, and thereafter, another male child was born. In this case, Rabbi Akiva prevailed in stating that the child born after miscarriage is not considered firstborn. The same rule applies to a kosher animal giving birth through a Cesarean section. It will not be considered firstborn, and it would not have to be redeemed by its owner.

- In another matter where an animal is firstborn, there is an exception in the Bible, which said that a donkey needs to be redeemed.

- Commenting on this rule, the donkey is not a kosher animal and it constitutes an exception. No reason given by the Torah on why only the donkey's first born must be redeemed.

- Following talmudic debates the sages remained in agreement with the Torah rule and hey concluded that the major rule was that only the donkey's firstborn should be redeemed and other non-kosher animals should not be placed in the category of dedicating the firstborn animal to God.

Tractate 44. Arakhin (evaluations) is pronounced *ah-rah-kheen*. This short tractate deals with evaluating property or wealth as a contribution or a gift to the temple. Everyone can make an evaluation or, as we say today, an estimate. An estimate can be made in money, property, and worth. While everyone can make an evaluation for himself or herself, the Bible, in the book of Leviticus 25 and Leviticus 27, excludes those people who are not capable of making an evaluation, such as those who are mentally challenged or physically limited, for the simple reason that, as the Mishnah says, they have no "understanding."

- For those who cannot afford to pay the actual currency or measure thereof, then the priest (the cohen) is the one to assess and decide what proportionate value or goods can be contributed in lieu of the set dues, such as if part of the land or the house should go toward the dues. Firstlings of animals do not count since they belong to God. The tithes from the land do not count toward the dues.

- The Bible in Leviticus expounds even more, as follows:

> But if one is too poor for your dues, he shall be presented before the priest, and the priest shall assess him; the priest shall evaluate him according to what the person

who pledges can afford . . . If he consecrates his land as of the Jubilee year, its assessment stands. But if he consecrates his field after the Jubilee, the priest shall compute the price according to the years which are left until the Jubilee year, and its assessment shall be so reduced [from the value of the field] . . . But a firstling of animals which [normally] belongs to God cannot be consecrated by anybody [to the sanctuary, as gift or dues]; whether ox or sheep, it is the Lord's . . . All tithes of the land, whether seed from the ground or fruit from the tree, are the Lord's; they are holy to the Lord. (Leviticus 27:8, 18, 26, and 30)

Tractate 45. *Temurah* or exchange speaks about sacrificial cattle. It is pronounced *teh-moo-rah*. The Mishnah concurs with the Bible when it comes to forbidding exchanging a dedicated animal (for sacrifice) with another animal. As it is said in Leviticus 27:

> One may not exchange or substitute another for it, either good for bad, or bad for good . . . All tithes of the herd or flock, of all that passes under the shepherd's staff, every tenth one, shall be holy to the Lord. He must not discriminate between good and bad or make substitution for it.

Tractate 46. Keritot (plural of *karet)* or divine punishment is pronounced *keh-ree-tot.* It means, literally, "cut off." The Mishnah in this tractate lists thirty-six transgressions for which a man or a woman are cut off from the community. Talmudic scholars go one step further and interpret that punishment of karet as one not having a future in the world to come if those transgressions are deliberately committed.

- The serious sins center around incest and having intercourse with blood-related relatives (father, mother, sister, brother) and having intercourse with animals. More serious sins are desecrating the Sabbath and the holidays, including Yom Kippur (the most solemn holiday), and eating leavened bread on the Passover holiday. The other sins listed center around biblical and postbiblical times when the temple still existed.

- Most of the sins cited above involve human behavior and are already considered immoral today. Some of them result in a severe fine or a harsher punishment.

- The Mishnah states that those sins are subject to severe punishment if they are committed intentionally. For those sins committed unintentionally, a sin offering is brought to the temple

Tractate 47. Meilah or inadvertent sin is pronounced *meh-ee-lah*. It is a tractate speaking about a transgression done in sacred things. Examples of meilah do not seem to be clear or specific in the Mishnah as well as in the Bible. However, we can cite a modern example: if a congregant profited by borrowing an item from the temple with the intention of soon returning it but forgot to return it, it can be considered as meilah. The Mishnah says that if a man derived a perutha's worth [equivalent to today's penny] from Temple property, even if he did no lessen its value, he is guilty of Meilah. (Meilah 5:1)

This was according to Rabbi Akiba.

The Bible says in Leviticus, concerning this transgression,

> if anyone commits a trespass and sin through error in the holy things of the Lord . . . he shall make restitution for that which he has done amiss in the holy thing and shall add the fifth part . . . and give it to the priest; and the priest shall make atonement for him with the ram of the guilt offering, and he shall be forgiven. (Leviticus 5:15–16)

- The Mishnah gave examples of sins, which could not possibly be considered a sin in modern times. However, in temple times, any small thing committed, even inadvertently, could be considered a sin or, in mishnaic language, a sacrilege.

- Nevertheless, we can learn in modern times that it is imperative for any constituent or member of any contemporary temple to always contribute and never profit from anything regarding the temple.

Tractate 48. Tamid means "daily" and speaks about the daily sacrifice. It is pronounced *tah-meed*. This tractate describes the priestly duties in preparing for the daily sacrifice. The procedure is clear and concise. Preparations are made by the priests, in preparing the fire, the male lamb, and the blessings around the sacrifice.

- The daily offerings and the Sabbath offering were done regularly, the Sabbath offering always being of special nature. In this tractate, the Mishnah describes the priestly duties as it was prescribed in the Bible as follows:

  [God spoke to Moses about daily and Sabbath sacrifices as follows]... This is the fire offering you shall present to the

Lord: male lambs of the first year without blemish, two each day, for a perpetual burnt offering. One male lamb you shall present in the morning and the second male lamb you shall present at dusk. And the tenth of an *ephah* of fine flour for a meal offering mingled with a fourth part with a *hin* of beaten oil ... [That perpetual burnt offering was offered at Mount Sinai] as a pleasing odor, an offering to the Lord. And on the day of the Sabbath, two male lambs, being one year old, without blemish, and two-tenths of flour mingled with oil and with its drink offering. This is the burnt offering of every Sabbath, besides the perpetual burnt offering and the drink offering. (Numbers 28:3–9)

- This tractate of the Mishnah also tells us that the priests sang every day (morning and evening) a psalm for each day as follows: On the first day (Sunday) they sang Psalm 24. On the second day (Monday), they sang Psalm 48. On the third day (Tuesday), they sang Psalm 82. On the fourth day (Wednesday), they sang Psalm 94. On the fifth day (Thursday), they sang Psalm 81. On the sixth day (Friday), they sang Psalm 93. Finally, on the Sabbath, which is the seventh day, they sang Psalm 92.

- Incidentally, those songs are recited daily in every conservative and orthodox synagogue worldwide.

Tractate 49. Middot or measurements is pronounced *meed-dot*. It speaks about the measurements and the size of the temple. This was the second temple, which was built by Herod the Great. Although Herod was considered a mean dictator, he is given credit by all Bible and history scholars to have done a magnificent job in rebuilding the second temple, which was comparable in size to King Solomon's first temple.

- "The Temple mountain was five hundred cubits by five hundred. The largest part faced south, the next largest toward the east, the third northward, and the smallest was to the west. The largest part was the most used" (Middot 2:1).

- We see how the Temple was briefly described. There are no commentaries by the Mishnaic and the Talmudic scholars about those measurements. The Herod Temple or second temple lasted eighty-nine years, from 19 BCE to 70 CE when the Romans destroyed it.

Tractate 50. Kinnim or bird offering is pronounced kee-neem. The word originates from the word *ken*, which is a nest. It is understood to be a pair of turtledoves to be brought to the priest. One bird is for olah (freewill offering), and the other bird is for hattat (sin offering).

- The hattat or sin offering is brought when a person has been cured from a disease or a woman has just given childbirth and she has been purified. This offering has been previously mentioned for committing an unintentional sin.

- The doves or birds were given in lieu of a larger, more costly sacrifice such as a cow, a bull, or a sheep.

- The hattat was to be offered first, then the olah came in second. The following is the detailed biblical quote about a woman giving birth and the bird offering (kinnim):

> [God said to Moses] Speak to the Israelite people, saying, "When a woman conceives and gives birth to a male child, she shall be impure for seven days . . . On the eighth day, the flesh of his [referring to the male baby] foreskin shall be circumcised. For thirty-three days, she shall remain in a state of blood purification. She is not to touch any consecrated thing nor enter the sanctuary until her period of purification is completed. If she gives birth to a female, she shall be impure for two weeks . . . and she shall remain in a state of blood purification for sixty-six days. When the days of her purification are completed, for either son or daughter, she shall bring to the priest, at the entrance of the

Tent of Meeting, a lamb in its first year for a burnt offering, and a pigeon or a turtledove for a sin offering . . . And the priest shall make atonement for her, and she shall be clean."(Leviticus 12:2–8)

- The following is the another self explanatory quote on the same subject from tractate Kinnim:

If a woman said: "I pledge myself to bring a pair of birds if I bear a son, and she did bear a son, she must bring two pairs, one for her vow and one for her obligation." (Kinnim 3:6)

Based on biblical instructions, a woman giving birth to a male waits thirty-three days before she is considered purified. In case of a female child, a mother waits sixty-six days before entering the sanctuary. Thus, we learn a Hebrew woman is welcome to the sanctuary but only after the purification mentioned above.

Chapter Twelve

Tohorot (Pronounced *To-Hoh-Rot* or *To-Hah-Rot*) Translates into Purities or Cleanliness

The Sixth and the Last Order of the Mishnah

This order includes the largest number of tractates, and it deals with clean and unclean matters in regard to people as well as objects. A vessel can be contaminated if a man who touched a dead body touched that vessel. The same applies if a man touched a dead animal.

It also deals with plagues or leprosy and how it is approached by the high priest or member of the temple who decides when a man is clear of leprosy.

This order also touches on purity and impurity for women. Usually women use the mikvah (mikveh) to purify themselves with water following their menstrual cycle or after giving birth.

In order to understand better this order, we have brought numerous quotes from the Bible, on which the Mishnah and the Gemarah rely, in order to make their arguments about cleanliness and impurity.

The following passages are biblical quotes and commentaries supporting this Talmudic tractate on purity. The priest in biblical times acted as a health specialist, and it was only by his approval that a man or a woman could be declared clean after they contacted a disease or had been contaminated by touching impure objects.

The readers can either be impressed or overwhelmed with the lengthy biblical details on purity and impurity found in the upcoming quotes.

The Priest's Duty in Regard to Cleanliness

The priest examines a person who has visible symptoms of skin disease, and he decides on when that person is declared pure or impure to enter the sanctuary.

> The priest shall look at the [suspected] leprous spot on the skin of his body. If the hair in the spot has turned white

and the spot appears to be deeper than the skin of his body, it is a leprous affection. When the priest sees it, he shall pronounce him impure. But if this is a white spot in the skin of his flesh and it does not appear to be deeper than the skin and its hair did not turn white, the priest shall quarantine the spot for the seven days. And the priest shall see on the seventh day, and behold, the affection remains the same but did not spread into the skin. The priest shall isolate him [the affected man] for seven more days. And the priest shall see him again, on the seventh day, and behold, the leprous spot has healed and did not spread unto the skin. The priest shall declare him pure. It is a scab. He [the leprous] shall wash his clothes and become pure. (Leviticus 13:3–6)

The qualification of the leprous and infected people by the priest does not end here. The Bible goes on with descriptions of the affected areas in minute details, making a separation between healed and unhealed spot and between clean and unclean.

As we see here, the priest holds a role of medical importance as well as a health regulator. The health is directly tied to purity or lack of it. Therefore, only a pure and clean person can approach the holy venues. Consequently, the priest determines if leprosy or other skin conditions exist, as the following example shows.

> When the flesh has a fire burn on its skin and the cicatrix of the burn becomes a bright spot, reddish white, or white. And the priest shall look at it, and behold, it turned to white hair in the bright spot, and its appearance is deeper from the [surface of] the skin. It is [considered] leprosy. It has developed in the burn. The priest shall declare him unclean. It is a plague of leprosy. (Leviticus 13:24–26)

The same process as we have seen above continues. In an interval of seven days, the priest continues to check on the disease and the impurity. When the infection is declared clear by the priest on any physical condition, it is when a person is ready for the following phase, which is a ceremony confirming the state of purity and cleanliness. The number seven continues to have an influence on the frequency of visits.

> On the seventh day, the priest shall examine him. If it has spread in the skin, the priest shall pronounce him unclean; it is a plague of leprosy. (Leviticus 13:27)

> But if the priest finds that the scab infection does not appear to go deeper than the skin, yet there is no black hair in it, the priest shall isolate the person . . . for seven days. (Leviticus 13:31)

> On the seventh day, he shall examine the infection. If the infection has spread in the cloth . . . for whatever purpose the skin may be used, the affection is a malignant infection; it is impure. (Leviticus 13:51)

Men and Women Are Treated Equally

Men and women are treated equally in regard to purification (except for the purification mentioned above regarding the birth of a male or female child):

If a man or a woman has infection on the head or in the beard, the priest shall examine the infection. (Leviticus 13:29–30)

Hygiene Goes with the Ritual

Contaminated clothes should be burned or washed depending on the gravity of the case:

And if it seen again in the cloth, whether in warp or in woof, or in any article of skin, it is breaking out; the infected article shall be consumed in fire. And the cloth, the warp or the woof, or whatever skin connected that you shall wash and the plague departed from them, it shall be washed again, and it shall be pure.(Leviticus 13:57–58)

The above chapter on purification is tied to the following chapter in the Pentateuch called *metzorah,* which means "the leper." It seems that in ancient times, there was an emphasis on dealing with extreme infections such as leprosy.

There is a special ritual in dealing with the leper. Following the physical healing, the priest performs a twofold ritual, a symbolic one (involving bird sacrifice) and a more substantial ritual involving two male lambs and cedar wood:

> [When] the priest goes out of the camp and when the priest sees that the leper has been healed, the priest shall order and will take, for the person to be purified, two live clean birds, cedar wood, scarlet, and hyssop . . . On the eighth day, he shall take two male lambs without blemish, one ewe lamb in its first year without blemish, three-tenths of a measure of choice flour with oil mixed in for a grain offering, and one log of oil. These shall be presented before the Lord with the person to be purified at the entrance of the Tent of Meeting, by the priest who performs the purification . . . And of the oil left in his palm shall be put by the priest on the tip of the right ear of the one being purified, on the thumb of his right hand, and on the big toe of his

right foot, upon the blood of the guilt offering. The remnant of the oil in his palm the priest shall put on the head of the one being purified. Thus, the priest shall make atonement for him before the Lord. (Leviticus 14:3–4, 10–11, and 17–18)

If the Leper Cannot Afford a Lamb

Purification shows some flexibility as seen by this law about those who cannot afford to sacrifice a lamb:

And if he is poor . . . he shall take one male lamb for a guilt offering, to be presented for atonement on his behalf; one-tenth of a measure of choice flour with oil mixed in for a grain offering, and a log of oil, and two turtledoves or two pigeons, according to his means, the one to be the sin offering and the other the burnt offering. (Leviticus 14:21–22)

Oil Sprinkling Completes the Ritual

The oil ritual performed by the priest on the healed leper is the final step of purification, thus reinstating a Hebrew leper to normal entry to the sanctuary:

> And from the oil the priest shall then pour into the palm of the left hand of the priest, and with the finger of his right hand, the priest shall sprinkle some of the oil that is in the palm of his left hand seven times before the Lord . . . He shall then offer one of the turtledoves or pigeons . . . as a sin offering and the other as a burnt offering, together with the grain offering. And the priest shall make atonement for the one being cleansed before the Lord. (Leviticus 14:26–27 and 30–31)

The Priest May Also Inspect a Dwelling

In regard to leprosy, God instructs Moses and Aaron to inspect suspicious buildings in the future land of Canaan:

And the priest shall command that they [the people involved in the plague] clear the house before the priest enters to examine the plague so that nothing in the house may become impure; after that, the priest shall enter to see the house. When he sees [while inspecting] the plague, and behold, the plague is in the walls of the house [in form of] hollow streaks, greenish or reddish, and appearing lower than the wall, the priest shall then get out of the house, and he shall close the house for seven days. And when the priest returns after seven days, he sees that the plague has spread in the walls of the house. And the priest shall instruct to have the stones infected with the plague taken out and thrown out to the outside of the camp to an impure place. (Leviticus 14:36–40)

The same procedure done for the infected person is done to the infected building. After an interval of seven days, the priest comes and examines the house and its stones until he gets satisfaction that the house is clear of impurity. In the meantime, no one is allowed in the house without washing their clothes and cleaning themselves until the house is declared officially pure by the priest.

Bird Sacrifice: A Ritual for House Purification

Besides the hygienic measures taken to disinfect a building suspected of carrying leprous germs and disease, there is the ritual of the holy symbol of purification as instructed by God to Moses and Aaron:

> He [the priest] shall purify the house with the blood of the bird, the fresh water, the live bird, the cedar wood, the hyssop, and with the scarlet. He shall set the live bird free outside the city in the open country. He shall [then] make atonement for the house, and it shall be pure. This is the law [the rule] for every leprous infection or for a scab. [The same rule applies] for the leprous infection of a garment and for the house. (Leviticus 14:52–57)

Laws Involving Other Infections

Laws involving infected men and women besides leprosy and other skin infections are addressed. They apply to men and women within their relationships. Contamination is a dominating factor, and important steps are taken to avoid serious infections:

> A man who has a discharge issuing from his flesh, his discharge is impure. This shall be his impurity in this discharge. Whether his flesh runs with a discharge or stopped up without a discharge, it is [declared] impurity: Any bed on which the one with the discharge lies shall be impure, and every object on which he sits shall be impure. Anyone who touches his bed shall wash his clothes, bathe with water, and remain impure until evening. Whosoever sits on an object on which the one with the discharge has sat shall wash his clothes, bathe in water, and remain impure until evening. (Leviticus 15:2–6)

The Symbolic Bird Ritual Completes the Purification of Men and Women

> And on the eighth day, he shall take two turtledoves or two young pigeons and come before the Lord at the entrance of the Tent of Meeting and give them to the priest. And the priest shall offer them, the one as a sin offering and the other as a burnt offering. And the priest shall make atonement on his behalf, for his discharge, before the Lord. (Leviticus 15:14–15)

summarizing the above biblical quotes in regard to purity, we learned that while the purification process is a hygienic process, it is also accompanied by a ritual which serves as a symbol for sanctity. The same law of purification applies to buildings and dwellings.

The Mishnaic Version on Toharot (Purities)

The Mishnah discussed the laws of purification and cleanliness in the following tractates.

Tractate 51. Kelim is pronounced *keh-leem* and means "utensils" or "vessels."

- If a man touches a vessel that has been in contact with a dead man and another man touches the vessel or the article, the two men and the vessels are declared unclean. If a fourth man contact comes in contact with the contaminated vessel or the contaminated man, the verdict is lighter. The fourth man has to wait until evening to be declared pure and clear of contamination.

- *Avot hatuma* is a term in the Mishnah that means "the father of contamination." It is pronounced *ah-vot-hatum-ah*. It is a term used for extreme contamination, such as touching a human corpse, a dead animal, a leper, and the like.

Tractate 52. Oholot or tents is pronounced *oh-hah-lot*.

- If a man enters a tent where a dead man is found inside, the man is declared unclean. Every vessel in the tent, which is not hermetically sealed, shall also be declared unclean.

- It takes seven days to clear the contamination. If within those seven days, another man touches the contaminated man, he will have to wait until the evening to clear himself from contamination.

- If after seven days, the contaminated man was not found clear and pure by the official priest, then he will have to wait until he is declared clear.

- In another matter, this tractate discusses the timing in which a man can be pronounced dead. A man cannot be declared dead until his heart had stopped beating and, consequently, until his soul has departed. While agonizing, a man can still perform legal procedures like liberate someone from levirate marriage. Taking it further, a man on his deathbed can still manage matters concerning inheritance or business transactions until his soul has departed from him.

- Even an animal will not be considered dead until its soul has completely left.

- About kosher animals the Mishnah implied: If an animal's head is severed, even as the remainder of the animal still moves, the animal is declared non-kosher.

- The Mishnaic fathers were privy in human anatomy. They estimated that there are 248 parts of the body and each part is subject to defilement or contamination. However, a fleshy part of the body only qualifies for defilement within a tent. A bone alone does not qualify for contamination in a tent.

Tractate 53. Negaim, or leprosy, is pronounced neh-gah-eem. This tractate comments on the biblical quotes cited above as follows.

- As found in the Torah, leprosy is a serious source of contamination. It can be found in a human body, in a house, and in human clothing.

- The sages debated whether leprosy can be verified on any day that ends on the Sabbath day. One thing they agreed on: inspection on leprosy cannot be done on the Sabbath day.

- Leprosy is considered so serious that garments must be washed accordingly in order to avoid contamination:

> The hides of the creatures of the sea cannot contract the contamination of leprosy, but if one connected with them anything that grows on land . . . they, too, become susceptible. (Negaim 11:1)

Tractate 54. Parah is pronounced *pah-rah*. It means "cow," an allusion to "the red cow" or "red heifer." The Mishnaic sages were trying to understand the real meaning behind the ritual of the red heifer, which was supposed to help with purification. That practice of purification could not exist any longer after the destruction of the Jerusalem temple in the year 70 CE.

- The ritual of the red (brown) cow gave the sages many challenges as they debated about what was the exact color of the cow, how to slaughter it, how to burn it, how to make sure that the cow did not carry any burden so it would be as close to the instructions given by the Bible.

- Without explanation given to Moses by God, this ritual is complex but necessary. The brown cow is to be slaughtered and burned completely. Its ashes are to be collected and mixed with water, cedar wood, hyssop, and scarlet and will serve as "water of purification" to purify a person who touched a body, among other things.

- The person who burns the cow becomes impure for one day. Only a pure person, meaning a person who did not have contact with a dead body and who is free from any other contamination, can handle the process of mixing and preparing the purification waters:

> And he who performed the burning [of the cow] shall wash his clothes in water, bathe his flesh in water, and be impure until evening. A pure man shall

gather the ashes of the cow and deposit them outside the camp. And it shall be a safeguard for the community of children of Israel as water for sprinkling, as water for purification from sin. (Numbers 19:8–9)

Tractate 55. Tohorot is pronounced *to-ho-rot*. This tractate carries the name of the entire order of tohorot. It deals with clean and unclean objects and their contaminating other objects or other people. The following are the main points discussed by the sages in this tractate:

- If there is doubt about what someone touched, then the sages declared him clean because he had no intention of touching anything impure (although Rabbi Akiva declared him unclean, but his opinion was not accepted by the majority).

- Should a whole house be declared ritually unclean if someone who works in a house and is considered *am-haaretz* were asleep when the owner entered the house. Am-haretz is a term used to describe a person who is not familiar with the law and who is not privy with the details of purity and contamination.

- This could very well be a contemporary case when a worker who is employed by a religious family uses certain utensils he or she was not supposed to use.

- The sages declared that only those objects touched by the person should be declared unclean, not the whole house.

Tractate 56. Mikvaot is the plural of mikveh (mikvah), which means "ritual bath." It is pronounced *meekvah-ot*, and it literally means "cisterns" or "a pool of water", normally used for purification for men and women alike."

- The traditional ritual bath still exists today as it has been in existence since biblical and postbiblical times.

- It is usually designed for women following their monthly cycle, after giving birth, and just before getting married.

- If one is not sure if the actual volume of the mikveh is correct or if it is doubtful that he immersed himself properly, then the sages declared him unclean.

- All sea including inland seas (lakes) may serve as a mikveh except for those men and women who have an abnormal disease, such as leprosy, and women who, after their menstrual cycle, are still bleeding.

Tractate 57. Niddah or woman's cycle is pronounced *need-dah*. It speaks about a menstruating woman and how her purification takes place following her monthly cycle.

- From the time a woman discovers the blood flow, she will be impure for seven days, Afterward, she can purify herself in a mikveh.

- Following the monthly cycle and purification period, a woman is supposed to be ritually clean for intercourse unless there are other blood problems not related to the normal cycle.

Tractate 58. Makhshirim or koshering and rendering fit to consume or to touch. It is pronounced *makh-shee-reem.* This tractate deals with food that could become non-kosher (not ritually fit to consume).

- The sages said that food mixed with water can become unclean. This is not very clear because we use water all the time, accidentally or expressly. The sages are referring to a quote from Leviticus 11:34, 37, 38, which prohibits consumption of food if a carcass falls on a utensil and mixes with water. In that case, both the utensil and the food are unfit to eat.

- An exception to this rule is as follows: if a seed is about to be sown and a carcass falls on it, the seed is considered clean.

- The Mishnah, in this tractate, speaks about another subject, not directly connected with purification. If a child is abandoned in an all-Jewish area, he will be considered Jewish. If an abandoned child is found in a predominantly non-Jewish area, the child is considered non-Jewish. If the area is populated by half Jews and half non-Jews, then the child is considered Jewish.

Tractate 59. Zavim or bodily discharges is pronounced *zah-veem*. This tractate deals with bodily secretions, such as a contagious disease, which can contaminate other people.

- Anyone touching a man or a woman who has bodily discharge is unclean (see above the biblical quote in the introduction to Tohorot).

- The sages established safeguards around those people with an unusual contagious disease of men or women with bodily discharge. No one can ride with them in a boat or sit with them on a bench.

Tractate 60. Tevul yom literally means "immersed for one day." It is pronounced *teh-vool yom.*

- As we have seen before, in biblical quotes and in the Mishnah, some people are unclean for one day until evening. They are called tevul yom for a man and tevulat yom for a woman.

- The Talmudic sages elaborated further that

> a woman who is *tevulat yom* may knead dough, cut off the hallah, and set it apart. But she must put it . . . on a tray . . . for the dough she touched only suffered third-degree contamination. (Tevul Yom 4:2)

Tractate 61. Yadaim literally means "hands." It is pronounced *yah-dah-yeem*. It speaks about hygiene in hands, before eating or praying or doing anything that involves clean hands and performing a holy ritual.

- Although the Torah did not specifically speak about washing hands before eating or before performing a ritual commandment, ritual washing of the hands was practiced since biblical and postbiblical times. It was understood so because washing one's body or cloth in water is mentioned several times in the Bible.

- The sages discussed the way hands should be washed before any ritual and how much water should be used. While the rabbis did not always agree on the same method of washing hands, it is, fortunately, a way of life today. People wash hands before they eat and health care specialists wash hands or put on gloves before they perform anything in order to protect them from getting germs or spreading germs.

- In orthodox and some conservative families and congregations, people's handwashing before a prayer is done in three stages: pouring with right hand to left hand, pouring with left hand to right hand, and finally, pouring on both hand simultaneously before making the blessing on washing hands (left-handed people may use their left hand first).

Tractate 62. Uktzin or stalks is pronounced *ook-tseen*. This is the last tractate of the Mishnah. Some sages did not understand why this tractate was the last one in this order. On the other hand, other sages thought there was a good reason why it was placed last in the Mishnah. The reason being that it did not seem to have a direct connection to the Torah's commandments. Yet it is always important to quote the sages of the Mishnah who said in this tractate that

> when olive leaves are pickled with the olives, the leaves remain ritually clean, for pickling them was only for appearance's sake. The fibers of a cucumber and the sprouts on the end are ritually clean. (Uktzin 2:1)

Yet an encouraging blessing of peace concludes the Mishnah:

> The Lord will give strength to His people. The Lord will bless His people with peace. (Psalms 29:11)

One concluding thought on the above tractate is that in a world full of wars between nations and between countries, the last quote is very much in place to end such a deep and meaningful study of postbiblical sages. God's people are everyone on earth, and prayers are made in every faith to establish peace on earth. Every religion seeks to establish harmony between world states and between rival groups within the same country.

In order to complete the wisdom of the Mishnah, we have left room for one important tractate, Pirkey Avot, the maxims of the fathers, which will cover the next three chapters and which strictly deals with ethics, justice and human behavior.

THE TALMUD COVERS OVER 6200 PAGES

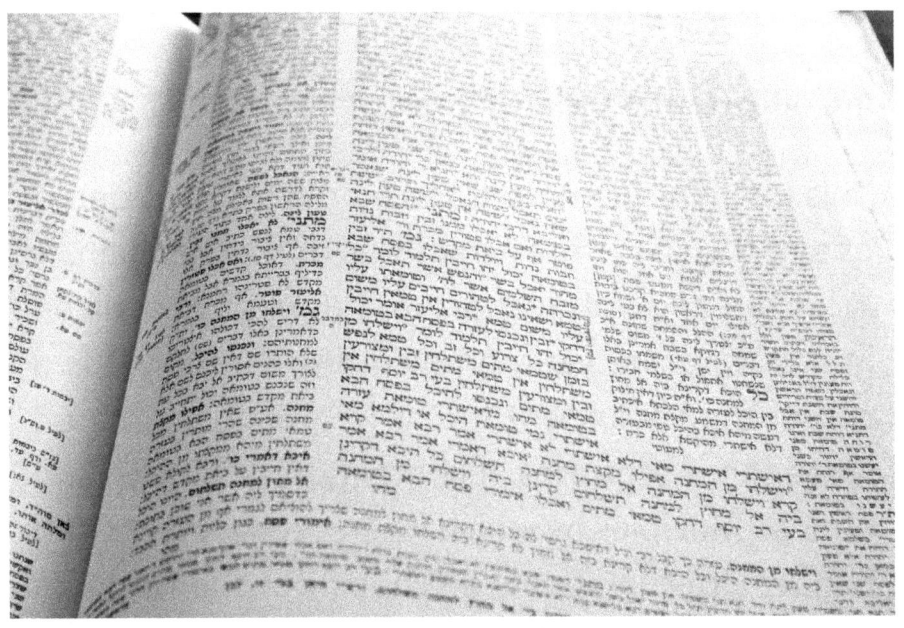

Chapter Thirteen

Pirkey Avot (The Wise Chapters of the Forefathers—Also Called the Ethics of the Fathers)

Introduction to Pirkey Avot

This precious document Pirkey Avot is considered one of the sixty-three tractates of the Mishnah. It is known as Avot in short and it was not written in one day, one year, or even one century. It is a compilation of ancient Jewish knowledge gathered throughout centuries. It contains basic human and ethical principles by which a person should act and behave. It is, in a way, a synopsis of the Mishnah and the Talmud. It is admired and revered by Jews and non-Jews alike.

Although Pirkey Avot touches on faith and God, it centers on ethics as a way of life. While we find countless quotes from the Bible in this book, we notice that the forty scholars quoted in this book direct the reader to a more modern way of looking into the scriptures.

Pirkey Avot preaches humility, simplicity, justice, and human discipline. No one should get too much credit for acquiring abundant knowledge and wisdom. Meaningful occupation must accompany the study of the Torah and its understanding. In order to be happy on earth, we must be true to ourselves because a certain divine force will be watching our behavior. Without always mentioning the name of God, the text underlines a constant divine presence.

The text includes maxims and phrases, which were compiled during a four-hundred-year span: from Simon the Just (200 BCE) all the way to Yehuda Hanassi (Judah the Prince), who achieved the compilation of six orders of the Mishnah (around the year 200 CE).

Synopsis of Pirkey Avot

Pirkey Avot was studied by many Jewish scholars (like Rabbi Marc Angel and Rabbi Lord Jonathan Sacks) and non-Jewish scholars (like R. Travers Herford). Incidentally, Rabbi Jonathan Sacks translated the Pirkey Avot from Hebrew (and Aramaic) to English (Koren Publishers, Jerusalem, 2015).

- There are six chapters in all in Pirkey Avot.

- The first five chapters quote the wisdom of the sages around the beginning of the first millennium, roughly two hundred years before and after the destruction of the second temple by the Romans (70 CE).

- The sixth chapter was added after the closing of the Talmud (500 CE).

- The first chapter describes how the Torah was transmitted from Moses to his successors and their successors.

- The book contains maxims preached by the Sadducees as well as by the Pharisees. The House of Hillel was headed by the Pharisees, while the House of Shammai was headed by the Sadducees.

- It tells us how the Torah was transmitted from Moses down to his successors as follows: Moses received the Torah from Mount Sinai, and he gave it to Joshua. From Joshua, the Torah was handed down to the elders. The elders handed it to the prophets, and the prophets handed it to the men of the Great Assembly. Simon the just was among the last members of the Great Synagogue (Hakeneset Hagedolah).

- Summarizing with further details, the Torah originated with Moses and, according to Pirkey Avot, was transmitted without interruption (following all stages mentioned above) to pairs (zuggot) of sages. The last pair was the combination of Hillel and Shammai. From there to Rabban Gamliel to Rabbi Shimon Ben Gamliel (the son of Gamliel) to Rabbi Yohanan Ben Zakkai. Rabbi Simeon Ben Gamliel and Rabbi Yohanan Ben Zakkai were under siege in Jerusalem when the Romans prepared to destroy the second temple (year 70).

- While Shimon Ben Gamliel was killed by the zealots who fought against the pacifist leaders of Jerusalem, Rabbi Yohanan Ben Zakkai managed to get out of the besieged Jerusalem in order to open new academies and educate new disciples in the city of Yabneh (Yavneh).

- Rabbi Yohanan gets the most credit for preserving the Jewish tradition by substituting temple sacrifices with Torah learning and prayers.

- This spiritual substitution, conceived and successfully implemented by Rabbi Yohanan, stands to be among one of the main reasons for the spiritual survival of the Hebrew and the Jewish culture.

- Rabbi Yohanan Ben Zakai will be spoken about frequently in this study. We learn that after he sent his students to research the best way one should conduct oneself under, the students came out with different choices. The choice made by Rabbi Yohanan was a good heart. The rabbi chose a good heart because a good heart included many aspects, and therefore, it is chosen over a good eye and other choices. A good heart within a person encompasses many good qualities. That conclusion was made after one of the students, Rabbi Eleazar Ben Arach went out to the world to research only to discover that a good heart was the best choice of what a human being should follow. Rabbi Eleazar was considered the brightest student at the time of his discovery. More on Rabbi Eleazar can be found in further comments.

The Importance of Avot in History and Jewish Rituals

- Several parts of Pirkey Avot are used in Jewish daily prayers.

- By the eleventh century CE, Pirkey Avot was read in synagogues in the Sabbath during the minhah or minha service, which is done in the afternoon.

- Rabbi Meir, another Avot icon, is featured in the sixth chapter of Pirkey Avot. His wisdom will be discussed below.

- The Avot work includes rabbis and scholars who lived before the year 70 CE (destruction of the second temple): Simon the Just, Shemayah and Avtatalion, Hillel and Shammai, Rabban Gamliel I, Rabbi Shimon Ben Gamliel.

- Among the scholars who are featured in Pirkey Avot and who lived after the destruction of the temple (year 70 CE) are Rabbi Yohanan Ben Zakkai, Rabban Gamliel II, Rabbi Eleazar Ben Azariah, Rabbi Eleazar Ben Arach, and Rabbi Haninah Ben Dosa, just to name a few.

- Other important figures who lived before the final rebellion against Rome, in the year 135 CE, were Rabbi Akiba (Akiva), Rabbi Tarfon, Rabbi Hananiah Ben Teradion, Nehorai, and Elisha Ben Abuyah.

- After the rebellion and the last Jewish resistance was crushed under the Romans, two important scholars rose and left a lasting impact on the Jewish way of life: Rabbi Shimon Bar Yohai and Rabbi Meir. Rabbi Shimon Bar Yohai was known for his brilliance and for being the precursor of the Zohar, the Jewish mysticism. Rabbi Meir was known for a great influence on his generation of scholars. One of his famous quotes referred to the importance of repentance. The latter can save the world in the eyes of Rabbi Meir.

- Other rabbis mentioned in Pirkey Avot but who lived between the end of the second century and the beginning of the third century were Rabbi Yehudah Hanassi, who assembled the orders of the Mishnah; Rabban Gamaliel Ben Yehuda; Rabbi Yehuda Ben Tema; and Rabbi Shimon Ben Eleazar.

- It is interesting to state that among two hundred tannaitic scholars mentioned in the Mishnah, only forty of them were chosen to be represented in Pirkey Avot.

- Many of the ethical remarks and recommendations mentioned in Pirkey Avot were stated as a result of the Roman occupation of the Holy Land.

- We conclude that most scholars mentioned in Pirkey Avot lived around the first century of the millennium. Nevertheless, the other 160 scholars not mentioned in Pirkey Avot remain the inspiring icons in the Talmud. We saw earlier that the Mishnah and Gemarah (the Talmud) included about two hundred scholars in all.

Solomon Elkayam death certificate: before he died he preached love, peace,justice and loving-kindness

משרד הפנים מדינת ישראל

תעודת פטירה

שם המשפחה	אלקיים	השם הפרטי	סלמאן
שם הפרטי של האב	מסעוד	מספר הזהות	6 1 8 7 7 6 1
תאריך הלידה הגריגוריאני	שנה 1902	חודש 4	יום 15
המין זכר	המצב האישי נשוי	הלאום יהודי	הדת יהודית
תאריך הפטירה הגריגוריאני	שנה 1977	חודש 3	יום 2
תאריך הפטירה העברי	יום י"ב	חודש אדר	שנה תשל"ז
נפטר ב-	שם הישוב מסעף	שם בית החולים	
סיבת הפטירה			

הנני מאשר כי הפטירה נרשמה בפנקס הפטירות לשנת 1977

והתעודה ניתנה בהתאם לסעיף 30 (ב) לחוק מרשם האוכלוסין, תשכ"ה 1965

הוצאה במשרד הפנים ב מסעף בתאריך 16-3-77

חתימת פקיד רישום פטירות

צ. שורצבורד

מר/94 700x100 (4.76)

Chapter Fourteen

Who's Who in Pirkey Avot?

As we hinted before, Pirkey Avot quotes the Talmud and comes to concise conclusions, based on the lengthy and heated debates made in the Mishnah and Gemarah between scholars.

- As an introduction to this subject, it is important to mention Talmud Yoma (9b), which is one the tractates of the Mishnah. It says that the temple was destroyed as a result of baseless hatred (sin'at hinnam) between brethren. This can apply to the first and the second temple in Jerusalem. The rabbis cited in Pirkey Avot preach peace between people, tolerance, love, justice, and ethics, as we shall see below.

- Rabbi Tarfon, from the House of Shammai, was known for his humility and wise sayings: one of them was that we need not finish the job but we should keep on working and studying. His famous saying was that "the day is short and the task is great and the workers lazy . . . and the boss is pressing." He was also known for allowing to extinguish a fire on the day of the Sabbath if holy Torah scrolls were caught in a fire. Rabbi Tarfon, together with Rabbi Akiva, was one of five scholars mentioned in the Passover Haggadah who spent the night of the Seder talking about the exodus from Egypt. The story of Egypt was discussed all night and so passionately that the five scholars were reminded by their students that it was time to recite the morning prayer.

- Rabbi Hanina Ben Hakinai was a contemporary of Rabban Yohanan Ben Zakkai and Rabbi Akiba. He was one of ten martyrs cruelly murdered (just as Rabbi Akiba was) by the Romans after the rebellion of Bar Kochbah (135 CE).

- Rabbi Nehuniah Ben Hakanah was a contemporary of Rabban Yohanan Ben Zakai. He was also one of the authors of the kabbalah (Jewish mysticism). We stated before that Rabbi Shimon Bar Yohai is the precursor of the kabbalah. Rabbi Nehuniah was a prosperous and generous person who believed that the study of the Torah "spared the yoke of government and the yoke of worldly responsibilities." He is mentioned in the tractates of Megila and Berakhot of the Mishnah.

- Rabbi Haninah Ben Dosah was a contemporary of Rabbi Akiba. He stressed the importance of having ten people (or more) in a congregation as the spirit of God resides within them. He also stressed the importance of deeds over wisdom. He used to say that a person with good nature and good character is a person favored by God Himself.

- Rabbi Elazar of Bartota was the teacher of Rabbi Shimon Bar Yohai and Rabban Gamliel II. He professed that all and everything belongs to God. Therefore, charity is something we humans return to God by giving it to the proper people because it is His.

- Rabbi Meir was a student of Rabbi Akiba. He was also a teacher of Rabbi Yehuda Hanassi.

The above three scholars are often quoted as they greatly contributed to the Jewish heritage. Rabbi Meir was one of the most pacifist scholars in the Talmud. He remained a close friend with Elisha Ben Abuyah, his teacher, who became a heretic. Although Ben Abuyah abandoned the Jewish religion, culture, and way of life and cooperated with the ruling Romans against the occupied Jews, Rabbi Meir remained faithful to him.

Rabbi Meir preached learning the Torah for its own sake and not for show. The Torah brings out love of God and people, happiness, wisdom, friendship, humility, and forgiveness.

His teachings and those of Rabbi Akiba became among the most quoted in the Mishnah. Later on, Rabbi Yehudah the Prince (Hanasi) gathered all the teachings of all the scholars and created the six known books of the Mishnah. Rabbi Meir preached about reducing business dealings for the benefit of Torah study. He urged humility before every person. He explained that if one neglects the study of the Torah, he would find many more people who do the same. On the other hand, if a person works hard in studying and absorbing the Torah, there is a great reward waiting for him. So many praises were written on Rabbi Meir. However, some worth mentioning are about his love for the Holy Land. He used to say,

> One who lives in the Land of Israel and speaks the holy language is assured of his share in the world to come. (Shekalim 3:4)

Rabbi Meir is often quoted about the importance of repentance. He used to say, according to the sixteenth tractate, Yoma, concerning Yom Kippur that 'On account of an individual who repents, the sins of the whole world are forgiven.'

- Rabbi Dosa Ben Harkinas was a contemporary of Rabbi Yohanan Ben Zakkai in the academy of Yavneh. He did not favor sleeping late in the morning. He also advised against consuming alcohol in midafternoon. Although he forbade chats with children and ignorant people, that advice does not seem to hold in today's twenty-first century.

- Rabbi Elazar the Modaiite was a contemporary of Rabbi Yohanan Ben Zakkai. He was against desecrating holy things and holy matters, such as tefillin, tallit, biblical festivals, and all that is holy in the Jewish religion.

  One important advice, which agrees with our modern culture of the twenty-first century, is that he was definitely opposed to one person embarrassing another person in public. This advice remains so relevant in our days. He was also against falsifying the meaning of the precepts of the Torah. What he meant by that was that it was wrong to interpret the commandments of the Torah without consultation with a rabbinical authority.

- Rabbi Ishmael was a contemporary of Rabbi Akiba. He, like Shammai (the head of the Sadducees), recommended that we should greet every person cheerfully. Rabbi Ishmael was, unfortunately, one of the martyrs who were cruelly murdered by the Romans following the rebellion of Bar Kochbah (135 CE).

- Rabbi Akiba was a student of Rabbi Yehoshuah and Rabbi Eliezer. He was considered a leading interpreter of the Torah around the time of the rebellion against the Romans in 135 CE. Because he defied the Roman authorities who forbade all Jewish scholars to promote the teaching of the Torah, he was apprehended and tortured to death after the rebellion. He was the precursor of "fences to the Torah." This means, for example, if the Torah forbade committing adultery, Rabbi Akiba established rules that prevented a man from speaking in length to a woman so that it would not lead to immorality prescribed by the Torah.

This idea of the "fence to the Torah" is included in the Halachah. Thus the oral Torah, given along with the written Torah, served as a check and balance to the written Torah. Rabbi Akiba was, therefore, the master of Halachah. He also spoke about the tithes being a fence to a person's wealth. Silence, in the eyes of Rabbi Akiba, was the fence protecting wisdom. This does not mean that a wise scholar needs to observe silence all the time. This means that the wise person speaks when necessary while insisting on listening more than speaking.

Rabbi Akiba used to say, "Beloved is the man who was created in the image of God." He cited quotes from Genesis and Deuteronomy respectively, saying, "Because in the image of God, He made man; you are the children of the Lord, your God."

Furthermore, Rabbi Akiba made a deep statement about the destiny of man and justice in the world: While everything is foreseen in life, a person can make a choice to do well or choose evil ways. People's deeds are watched, whether they are good or bad deeds. Men and women can do anything they want in this world, but at the end, if the good deeds exceed the bad deeds, a person may have a place in the world to come. As Rabbi Akiba puts it,

the shop is open, the shopkeeper extends credit, the notebook [recording the deeds of man] is open, the hand writes. Whoever wishes to borrow can come and borrow and the collectors make rounds every day and collect payments whether a person knows it or not . . . the judgment is accurate and all is prepared for a banquet.

This is how Rabbi Akiba sees how people can carve their destiny.

- Rabbi Elazar Ben Azariah was one of the leaders of the Academy of Yavneh together with Rabban Gamliel. Rabbi Elazar repeats some of the ideas seen above about the fear of God. However, he juxtaposes the fear of God with wisdom, Torah and sustenance, knowledge and understanding. No quality can exist without the other. Knowledge of the Torah alone is not enough, according to Rabbi Elazar Ben Azariah. The result obtained from the above qualities is performing good deeds, and the conclusion is that deeds must exceed wisdom.

- Rabbi Elazar Ben Hisma was also a disciple of Rabban Gamliel. He is quoted in the Talmud (Horayot 10:1) as being well versed in astronomy and mathematics. Combining Torah and science, he spoke about bird offerings and menstrual periods to be calculated according to law. Astronomy and mathematics mean wisdom. They do not contradict the spirit of the Torah.

This is a rare time for us to see how a scholar from the academy of Yavneh speaks about scientific things we would be talking about in our century.

- Ben Zoma was not titled rabbi, but he was known for being extremely bright in interpreting scriptures. His first name was Shimon, and he was a student of Rabbi Yehoshuah. He professed that a wise man is the one who learns from everyone. He quoted the book of Proverbs to show that a wise man is the one who is eager to learn from everyone. He also learned from the book of Proverbs that the mighty person is the one who can control himself. He also said that, while leaning on the book of Psalms and the book of Samuel, a happy man is the one who is content with what he has or possesses. An honorable person is a person who respects other people.

- Ben Azzai was a contemporary of Ben Zoma. Shimon Ben Azzai was his full name. He was an important member of the Yavneh Academy, and he was a student of Rabbi Yehoshua. He taught that a minor mitzvah (good deed) was as important as a great one. People should make the same effort to perform both forms of good deeds. He also taught that performing one mitzvah leads to another mitzvah and committing one sin leads to committing another sin. He recommended being courteous to everyone. He taught people to never despise, hate, or misjudge the value of anyone "because there is no one who does not have his hour, and you cannot find a thing that does not have a place." He meant by that, that no one person should be underestimated, whether or not he or she is versed in the Torah, because everyone could have a special human character regardless of Torah knowledge.

- Rabbi Levitas was also a member of the Yavneh Academy. He preached about being extremely humble because our end is to be buried and be eaten by worms. Rabbi Levitas implied that humility found in our ancestors, Abraham, Isaac, Jacob, Moses, and Aaron, is necessary for a human being in order to be close to God Himself.

- Rabbi Yohanan Ben Beruka was another scholar who warned people not to profane the name of God. While desecration of the name of God in public is already forbidden, Rabbi Yohanan Ben Beruka thought that some people might desecrate the name of God in secret. That is also a transgression. What he meant by that was that some people could secretly do things not acceptable by the Torah or the Halakhah. Such behavior constitutes a desecration of God's name, whether it is done expressly or secretly.

- Rabbi Ishmael(another Rabbi Ishmael), the son of Rabbi Yohanan Ben Beruka, was a contemporary of Rabbi Meir and Rabbi Shimon Bar Yohai. He professed that teaching the Torah as a profession was acceptable on one condition: the Torah teacher must live the way the Torah instructs the person. The teacher should serve as an example to his students, and his way of life should truly reflect the precepts of the Torah.

- Rabbi Tsadok was a contemporary of Rabbi Yohanan Ben Zakkai. His words are in agreement with what the sage Hillel professed, "Do not separate yourself from the community, and do not make of the Torah a crown for self-benefit." The Torah should be learned for the sake of loving God only. It is not a means to grandeur. He also cautioned against becoming one who would be among those who prepare the judges for a judicial matter. This could also be interpreted as warning to people to not act as lawyers when they are sitting as judges. We can definitely see here a clear separation between those who judge and those who advocate.

- Rabbi Yose was a student of Rabbi Akiva in the Yavneh Academy. His theme centers on the person who honors the Torah. That person is respected by all humankind. This is a departure in that Rabbi Yose implies that Jews and non-Jews would respect a learned person who honors the Torah in all its phases. Honoring the Torah also means practicing to the fullest what the Torah prescribes. It also means that one teacher of the Torah must serve as an example to his students in practicing all the mitzvoth (the commandments) written in the Torah.

- Rabbi Ishmael, another Rabbi Ishmael was the son of Rabbi Yose (see above). He did not live in Yavneh as his faher did but in the north of the Holy Land, in another academy in the town of Tzipori. Rabbi Ishmael spoke about the responsibility of a judge. Because judges are highly placed in the hierarchy of the Torah and its laws, judges should be cautious in what they say and what they decide. They could be accused of rendering the wrong verdict or favoring one party over the other. Therefore, Rabbi Ishmael stated that if a person abstains from assuming the role of a judge, he could spare himself "enmity, robbery, and perjury." Furthermore, a judge who is haughty in his teaching and judgment can be considered as foolish, wicked, and arrogant.

- This does not mean that competent judges should shy away from their task. This means that a judge has an enormous task before him, and he must render justice in such a manner that he could never be accused of favoritism, thus avoiding enmity. Rabbi Ishmael further stated that a judge should not act alone in his decisions. He should not impose his views on his colleagues. On the contrary, his decision should be discussed and shared, and the final decision should be made after careful deliberation between the members of the court.

- Rabbi Yonatan was a student of Rabbi Ishmael and a contemporary of Rabbi Akiba. Rabbi Yonatan literally stated that a person keeping the Torah while living in a state of poverty ends up keeping in wealth. His words can be interpreted this way: If a poor person treasures the Torah and studies it thoroughly, it gives him a sense of richness and abundance of spiritual happiness. On the other hand, if a rich man neglects the Torah, he will end up neglecting it in poverty. This can also mean that a rich man with many means may feel spiritually empty despite his wealth because he neglected the Torah.

- Rabbi Eliezer Ben Yaakov was a student of Rabbi Akiba. He was well-liked in his community because of his good nature and his wisdom. He professed that a person performing a mitzvah acquires an advocate or a defender. On the other hand, the people committing transgressions trigger the existence of an accuser. As many scholars often speak in parables, Rabbi Eliezer implied that it is best for a person to do as many good deeds as possible in a lifetime. As no one is perfect and anyone, even a sage, may inadvertently commit a sin, it is preferable to have the mitzvoth (good deeds) exceed the transgressions. Repentance is a great opportunity for humans to correct themselves and redeem their soul because we know from the Bible (Jonah's story) that God has always forgiven and restored humans when they repent.

- Rabbi Yohanan the Shoemaker (Hasandlar) was a disciple of Rabbi Akiba. He was born in Alexandria, Egypt. His remark came after the defeat of the Bar Kochbah Rebellion. The Romans crushed the rebellion, but the sages and scholars never lost hope. Rabbi Yohanan preached that every assembly, which is in the name of heaven, would be established in the end. This also implies that the assemblies existing after the Bar Kochbah Rebellion were not up to par with their ritual and scholastic functions. Nevertheless, they functioned for the sake of God, even as they were weak and scarce throughout the land. Their intentions to continue worshiping God and pursuing the study of the Torah in their feeble situation would enable them to become a permanent, vibrant assembly.

- Rabbi Mathitiah Ben Heresh (the son of Heresh) also experienced the defeat of the Bar Kochbah rebellion. He consequently fled to Rome. He said, "Greet people first before they greet you. Be rather a tail to lions, and do not become a head of foxes." His quote is slightly different from the current proverb, which was circulating in the Holy Land and Rome and which was "better be a head of foxes than a tail among lions." As Rabbi Mathitiah lived under foreign occupation, he urged people to be cautious in what they say and what they do while facing the Roman authorities.

- Rabbi Elazar Ben Shammua was well qualified to be on the list of the brightest scholars in his generation. First, he was the student of the famous teacher Rabbi Akiba. When he became an illustrious teacher, he taught, among other students, no other than Rabbi Yehudah Hanasi (Hanassi), the assembler and the redactor of Mishnah. Rabbi Elazar Ben Shammua had a special respect for his students, his colleagues, and his friends and more so for his rabbis and teachers. He viewed his teaching rabbis as those who upheld the laws of the Torah since the times of Moses himself. Therefore, proper respect was due to rabbis as well as to students who performed the enormous task of working hard in order to fulfill the biblical mitzvoth (commandments).

- Rabbi Yehuda was also a teacher to Rabbi Yehuda Hanasi. He himself was a student of Rabbi Akiba. Rabbi Yehuda taught that those who study the Torah and the Halachah must not make any mistakes of judgment.

Mistakes, even if done inadvertently, can lead to rendering a false judgment and can put one of the opposing parties in jeopardy.

- Rabbi Shimon Bar Yohai is known as the precursor of the Zohar. He is a most revered and quoted rabbi in the Jewish tradition. He emphasized the importance of three crowns: the crown of the Torah, the crown of priesthood, and the crown of kingship. He implied that the crown of kingship and priesthood can be transmitted from father to son, the crown of the Torah must be earned through hard study and a true way of observing its precepts and those of the Halakhah. All crowns, no matter how they were achieved, must earn the honor of achieving a "good name," in the words of Rabbi Shimon. More will be written on this special sage throughout this book.

- Rabbi Shimon Ben Nathanel, another Rabbi Shimon, was helpful in cautioning people to be careful when they pray. He used to say in Pirkey Avot, "Be meticulous with the reading of the Shema and with prayer. When you pray, do not make your prayer routine, but . . . a supplication before the Almighty, as it is stated [in the book of Joel], '. . . He is benevolent and merciful, slow to anger and abundant in loving kindness' . . . and do not be wicked in your own eyes."

- Rabbi Nehurai is a pseudonym of Rabbi Elazar Ben Arach. We have seen earlier that he was the favorite student of Rabbi Yohanan Ben Zakkai. He was also a disciple of Rabbi Tarfon. We learned that Rabbi Eleazar went away from the academy of Yavneh and settled in Emmaus, another city in the Holy Land. He advises us that we must seek the Torah because the Torah is not going to seek us. He advises remaining with Torah associates and supporting them. By doing so, the study of Torah can flourish in the place of study. On the other hand, by being away from your original place of study and staying in another place, you might misinterpret some Torah precepts, and that will be wrong. In another study about the title Nehurai, we learn that that pseudonym was given to other bright scholars like Rabbi Meir.

- Rabbi Yanai is mentioned only once in the Pirkey Avot and the Mishnah. Rabbi Yanai comes with a very intriguing statement about the just people and the wicked people. While we humans expect righteous people to be rewarded in this world and the wicked people to be punished, Rabbi Yanai comes with his maxim, implying that we humans have no way of knowing why justice is not always rendered in this world. Perhaps justice could be rendered in the world to come whereby the righteous person is rewarded and the wicked one is punished. Contemporary writers like Rabbi Kushner wrote about when good things happen to bad people and bad things happen to good people.

- Rabbi Yaakov was reported in the Mishnah to be one of the teachers to Rabbi Yehuda the Prince (Hanassi). We learn from him to never interrupt a prayer when one encounters beautiful scenery while walking and praying simultaneously. In this other case, Rabbi Yaakov challenges us to be extremely aware that the good deeds performed in this world will introduce us to a better place in the world to come. He named this world to be a hallway leading to an illustrious *traklin,* which is a non-Hebrew word meaning "a banquet hall" (an allusion to a special hall waiting for righteous people in the world to come). He also said that better one hour of repentance and good deeds in this world than the entire life in the world to come. Did he mean that the world to come is not as important as one hour of good deeds in this world? Perhaps not. He implied that a person should be busy doing good deeds in this world because he or she may not have the chance to do so in the world to come. This does not contradict what he said above, namely that the good deeds we do in this world introduce us to other good things in the world to come.

• Rabbi Shimon Ben Eleazar was a colleague of Rabbi Yehuda Hanassi and a student of Rabbi Meir. He was very careful in cautioning us about the timing of things. He said, for example, not to try to calm your friend in the middle of his anger. Do not try to console someone while his dead relative or friend is lying in front of him. Do not bother to speak about a vow to your friend while he is making a pledge. He also advised to give space to a friend who is in the middle of his (or her) demise. This does not mean neglecting a friend. It means that it is advisable to give some time to a friend when he or she is going through a rough time. These are rules of behavior we understand in our century. They were good then, and they are still valid today.

- Samuel the Young or Shemuel Hakatan (the young one) was a precocious learner and a gifted scholar. In fact, Rabban Gamliel, head of the Assembly, appointed him to compose a blessing against the heretics. That blessing is included in daily Jewish prayers, recited three times a day. Some scholars at that time turned to heresy. One good example was Elisha Ben Abuyah. Elisha was first highly placed in the hierarchy of the elders and scholars. He was, in fact, a colleague of Rabbi Akiva and a previous teacher of Rabbi Meir. He turned into heresy and left the circle of Jewish scholars. Because there was a scholastic connection between Rabbi Meir and Elisha Ben Abuyah, the composers of Pirkey Avot allowed his name to be included in the book. Ben Abuyah said that studies done at a young age are compared to ink written on a new paper. On the other hand, studies done at an old age are compared to ink written on blotted paper. Samuel the Young also spoke about how we should treat our enemies. He repeated the words of King Solomon in the book of Proverbs (24:17–18) to be careful not to rejoice when your enemy falls or is destroyed. Since all humans are creatures of God, Samuel implied, being happy following your enemy's demise could make God angry.

The abovenamed rabbis and Talmudic scholars were among hundreds of scholars who contributed to Jewish wisdom during the mishnaic period, which extended for hundreds of years.

We found that many of their thoughts, maxims, and advice seem to be understood in our modern twenty-first century.

Things like justice, morality, knowledge, care for others, patience, perseverance, humility, and many more qualities are something we continue to observe today if we want to be successful.

Chapter Fifteen

Relevance of Pirkey Avot in the Twenty-First Century

When you read and reread the maxims of Pirkey Avot, you could assume that those rabbis and scholars who wrote them or discussed them could be living among us in the twenty-first century. They speak about law and order, humility versus arrogance, honesty or lack of it, education and ignorance, and fear to do evil and wisdom to control human behavior.

Pirkey Avot seems to represent the essence of how a person should behave, regardless of religion or faith.

Hereby, after careful analysis, we have assembled the maxims of Pirkey Avot, and we have grouped them into subjects and categories as follows:

- *The Torah must be accompanied by an occupation.* The rabbis in Pirkey Avot wanted to make sure that everyone had an occupation while emphasizing the importance of learning the Torah. Most scholars had another job besides being involved in the Torah. They were shoemakers, vendors, growers, land or real estate owners. Many of them belonged to the aristocracy. Several rabbis taught that it is not enough just to be a learned person. It is important to have a side occupation and deal with worldly matters as well. The intention to save time and be efficient in labor is not solely for work but also for studying the Torah.

- Rabbi Eleazar urged us to work and labor in what we do, including being spiritual, without expecting to finish the job. He never thought that one could finish his task. It would be almost impossible as the task is so great. This is a typical trait where parents teach their children and rabbis transmit their knowledge and legacy to their students for generations and generations. Rabbi Eleazar—who, according to the Talmud, was given another name (that is Rabbi Nehurai).

- He also suggested in another part of Pirkey Avot that the Torah is so important that one could exile himself to a remote place and keep on studying it. He also stressed that we should not assume that it will come after us (Avot 4).

To clarify this, Rabbi Elazar, at one point in his life, kept away from the Torah and withdrew to another place where he stopped learning the Torah and concentrated on other material things. The Talmud does not specify what material things he concentrated on. When he met his colleagues again, they realized that his knowledge was so low that they prayed for him to retrieve his wisdom. The name *Nehurai* suggests light or illumination; it is also derived from the word *nahar,* a flowing river. That title was also given to Rabbi Meir, who was also one of the brightest scholars in his time. More will be said about Rabbi Meir in this project. When Rabbi Elazar returned to the academy after a long absence, he came back to be the light for his colleagues and let his knowledge flow like a river.

A most important thing to say about the Torah is that most scholars agree that it was not given to them or to anyone as an inheritance. The Torah is considered a spiritual and intellectual asset to be absorbed, studied, and observed. It is transmitted from father to son and from teacher to student.

- *How to deal with the governing authorities.* In general, Pirkey Avot does not encourage anyone involved in the Torah to be associated with the governing authorities. There are special reasons for that. One main reason is the fact that the Holy Land had been occupied by foreign powers since the destruction of the first temple (586 BCE). The Babylonians, the Assyrians, the Persians, the Greeks, and the Romans left an impact on the occupied Jews. The only liberation the Jews felt in their land was the freedom to study the Torah and be closer to God. As long as they believed in a supreme power through their love of the Torah, they felt the yoke of an earthly government a lot less. Having God as their master made it easy for them to tolerate a ruling secular government. On this subject,

Rabbi Nehuniah Ben Hakkana said that "anyone who takes on himself the yoke of the Torah, they remove from him the yoke of kingdom and the yoke of worldly occupation" (Avot 3:6).

- A special warning about befriending people within governing authorities. Rabban Gamliel, the son of Judah the Prince, said to be careful about how you deal with the ruling authorities. In this case, it is certainly about the Roman authorities occupying the Holy Land for centuries before and after the Common Era. It says clearly,

> Be cautious of the authorities, for they do not make advances to a person except for their own needs. They seem friendly in their hour of advantage but they do not stand by a man in an hour of his crisis. (Avot 2:3)

The above warning can be attributed to any government, either an occupying force or especially a government in time of peace like in any democratic country. A perfect example can be seen right here in the United States where those politicians who want to be elected cater to their constituents in order to get their votes and financial support. Whether they always keep their promise is another thing.

- *Talk less and do more*. Shammai, head of the Sadducees, joined several other rabbis in urging people to talk less and do more. Some scholars in Pirkey Avot have concluded that good deeds are even better than wisdom itself. They feel that doing good deeds already include wisdom. Therefore, good deeds are better than wisdom. Shammai simply said "say less and do more" (Avot 1:15).

- Rabbi Shimon Ben Gamliel, a most revered spiritual leader and a martyr who was killed by the Romans for promoting the Torah, also spoke about the golden silence as being the ultimate sign of wisdom. He said,

  All my life I grew up among the sages and I found nothing better for the body than silence. Talk is not the chief thing but action is.

Whosoever talks too much brings sin. (Avot 1:17)

- *You must help yourself.* Rabbi Hillel the Great was the head of the Pharisees in the Holy Land, and he is one of the most quoted in Pirkey Avot. Among many things he preached was action as Shammai preached, but in a different way. In this case, Hillel urged people to take the initiative and fend for themselves about everything they believe in. He urged people to do the right thing right now and not wait any longer. For example, he taught his students to pursue peace, love their fellow people, bring them closer to the Torah, stay away from too much self-glorification, study the Torah, and help the poor and the deprived. He meant to do it without delay as he is quoted as saying,

  If I am not for myself, who will be? And if I were only for myself what Am I? And if not now, when? (Avot 1–14)

- *Do things for the sake of heaven.* This is a concise rule of conduct, which is implied throughout Pirkey Avot. It involves a person being humble, performing good deeds without having to take much credit for himself or herself, helping the poor, doing justice, and more. It demands a strict observation of the rules of the Torah and especially being involved in a congregation (as Rabbi Hillel often urged his fellow people to join the community and not to set oneself apart from it). All those things should be done in the name of heaven. This means that people should do all those good deeds whether someone is watching them or not. It is a commandment to be done between man and God. Rabbi Yohanan Hasandlar (the Shoemaker) used to say on this subject the following:

> Every assembly which is for the sake of Heaven will end up surviving and every assembly which is not [established] for the sake of heaven will end its existence. (Avot 4:14)

This principle is so alive in the twenty-first century: we hear in the news about so many corporations who ended up closing their doors or being sued because their objectives turned out to be deceitful and damaging to their trusting investors and clients.

The term "for the sake of heaven" can be interpreted today as being fair and just to the other person, whether it is a personal friend or a business client.

- *Anything done in excess leads to evil and destruction.* Rabbi Hillel warned about doing anything in excess. Although the following quote could be relevant to today's way of life, it certainly was real during the first millennium when Rabbi Hillel was alive. Rabbi Hillel said,

> He who increases flesh, increases worms, the more possessions, the more worry, the more women, the more witchcraft, the more maidservants, the more lewdness, the more menservants, the more stealing. (Avot 2:8)

Rabbi Hillel added wise qualifying comments about the idea of excess. Some excesses are good for you, as follows:

> The more Torah, the more life, the more advice, the more understanding, the more charity, the more peace. He who ever acquired a good name acquired it for himself. If one person acquired things connected to the Torah, he acquired for himself life for the world to come. (Avot 2:8)

Most of the warnings Rabbi Hillel brought up can be well made today when we hear about Hollywood and corporate celebrities who have been accused of sexual harassment. On the other hand, we also hear many stories about those charities that help people help themselves in providing them with jobs and other incentives. Those good deeds can keep peace in their communities.

- *Be humble.* Pirkey Avot underlines the quality of humility in several parts of the text. Humility is stressed whether you are rich or a top scholar. Rabban Yohanan Ben Zakkai used to say, "If you studied much Torah do not take too much credit for yourself, for you were born for that [anyway]" (Avot 2:9).

Rabbi Levitas from the academy of Yavneh used to say, "Be extremely humble because the expected end of a man is the worm [after death]" (Avot 4:4).

In the realm of justice and legal matters, Rabbi Tzadok used to say, "Do not use [the laws of the Torah] as a crown for self-aggrandizement and as a digging tool" (Avot 4:7).

Rabbi Hillel the Great also said on this subject of humility, "Anyone who uses the Torah as a crown could fade away. Therefore, you learn [that] whoever profits from the words of the Torah could destroy himself in this world" (Avot 4:7).

Rabbi Meir also urged people to do everything in a state of humility to the point of doing less business and learning more Torah. He used to say, "Be humble before every person and if you have neglected the Torah you have many other matters of neglect against you. However, if you worked hard in studying the Torah, He [God] will have many rewards to grant you" (Avot 4:12).

- *Have a heart.* Rabbi Yohanan Ben Zakkai is known to be the main figure to have restored faith among the Israelites who despaired after the second temple was destroyed (70 CE). He learned from the scriptures that while sacrifices were normal during temple days, it was necessary to pray to God as ancestors Jacob and Hannah and many others did. He also knew that besides prayers and sacrifices, there are other important things in life such as doing good deeds and being straight with God, as the Prophet Isaiah and Prophet Micah urged. In this part of Pirkey Avot, Rabbi Yohanan Ben Zakkai sent his five students to explore the exterior world (out of the academy) and discover what was the best way one should choose in this life. Although four of the disciples reported good choices such as a good eye (of goodness and generosity), a good companion, a good neighbor, and the skill of predictability, Rabbi

Yohanan Ben Zakkai favored the choice of Rabbi Eleazar Ben Arach who said that a good heart within a person was the best choice in human nature.

Rabbi Yohanan preferred this view because he said that a good heart included all the above qualities. A good heart does more in matters of helping people, being compassionate, praying and being with the Lord, and being good to all creatures. A good heart also means being good with finances when someone borrows money and pays it back on time.

Rabbi Yohanan also sent his disciples to explore what was the worst way a man should stay away from. Again, Rabbi Eleazar Ben Arach prevailed in his choice when he found out that the evil heart was the worse choice a person can lean on. The choice of an evil heart, being in the wrong, as opposed to a good heart, stood out against all the other choices (according to Avot 2:10–14).

- *Control your temper.* One way of maintaining respect between two people or more is to control one's temper. It is said, "Let the honor of your fellow person be as precious as your own honor" (Avot 2:15).

In chapter 5 of Pirkey Avot, we find four different cases of temperament: the first two cases are (1) being easy to anger and easy to be pacified and (2) being hard to anger and hard to be pacified. The text tells us that the gain is canceled by the loss, meaning if someone is angered and easily pacified, he is in no advantage or disadvantage. Another situation where the advantage is canceled by its disadvantage exists in one person who is hard to anger and hard to pacify. The best situation is found in a pious man, someone who is hard to anger and is easy to pacify. The opposite qualities can be found in a wicked man, meaning that that person is easy to anger and hard to pacify.

Our sages were inspired by King Solomon's book of Proverbs about people who control their temper:

> He that is slow to anger is better
> than the mighty and he who rules

over his spirit [is better] that one who takes a city. (Proverbs 16:32)

The book of Avot puts the people who control their temper in a class by itself. They are considered heroes, according to Avot 4:1.

- *Do not be evil to yourself.* Rabbi Shimon, while asking us to pray from the heart, cautions us not to make our prayer as a fixed routine. Rabbi Shimon implied that those praying should feel positive about themselves so they can feel positive about other people. This takes us to the teachings of Rabbi Akiba who repeated the commandment of the Torah to "love your neighbor as yourself" (Leviticus 19:18).

  When people respect, honor, and take care of themselves, they can respect, honor, and take care of other people. For this Rabbi Shimon said explicitly, "Do not be wicked in your own eyes" (Avot 2:18).

- *What is the right path to follow in life?* This question was posed and answered by Rabbi Yehuda Hanassi (135 CE–217 CE).

He was known for his spiritual leadership and for his erudition among scholars and Bible interpreters. He was responsible for compiling all tractates of the Mishnah, and he left an impressive legacy on his disciples and followers for generations to come. His name in Pirkey Avot was simply *Rabbi.*

He asked, "What is the right way a person should choose?" and he answered that the right way was the one that is a glory to the people who do it and an honor [received] from other people.

He added,

> Be as careful about a light commandment as in a major commandment for, you do not know how the rewards of the commandments are given. Calculate the loss of a good deed against its reward and the price of a transgression against its loss. Contemplate three things and you will not come to transgression: Know what is above you, one eye

is looking and one ear is hearing and all your deeds are written in the book. (Avot 2:1)

Rabbi Yehuda Hanassi could well be alive today in cautioning humans to be just and righteous. While watching today's news on television or on an iPhone, we learn that transgressing people end up getting caught. Therefore, transgressions do not pay. Eventually, the so-called important people are displayed in the media and being accused for their crimes. We follow today's news, and we find out how some celebrities and icons end up losing their fame and fortune.

- *On education of children and adults.* In general, students who are bashful and do not ask questions to inquire about an issue in the Torah will never learn. On the other hand, a teacher who is too demanding or too strict cannot be efficient in teaching his students. This is another bright advice from Hillel the Great (based on Avot 2:6).

On another matter, other sages such as Elisha Ben Abuyah prefer that students learn at a young age. Older people may not be as absorbing as young students (according to Avot 4:25).

This opinion can be debated nowadays as many people at an old age switch careers and learn a new profession. We also find in student education that the best quality in learning is found in someone who learns quickly and forgets slowly (per Avot 5:16).

- *Be there when there is no one else.* Rabbi Hillel urges people to be there when they are needed to help other people, especially when other people in the congregation do not take the initiative. As Hillel always taught, each individual should become a part of the community. As a community, there is real strength. However, when some people in the community fail to stand for what is right, he urges us to "strive to be the man" (Avot 2:5).

- *Importance of honor.* Here Rabbi Hillel urges, as other scholars did, to stay away from self-glorification. Honor will come from other people, and it is incumbent upon everyone to remain humble and not seek to be famous.

In our century, we call this ephemeral fame "fifteen minutes of fame."

In order to be happy and remain respected by all people Hillel said, "He who makes worldly use of the crown . . . passes away" (Avot 1:13). This may not necessarily mean death for a self-glorified person, but it can be detrimental for people who claim too much credit for themselves, as we have watched in the news and on social media.

This implies that boasting about self-achievement, either in knowledge of the Torah and in other matters, is inadvisable. Actually, in the mind of Hillel, respect and honor are qualities that are awarded by the community to an individual and not by the individual to himself or herself.

Rabbi Hillel summarized this subject of honor in Aramaic, saying,

> Whoever uses the Torah as a crown may fade away. From this you learn that whosoever seeks personal benefit from the words

of the Torah withdraws his life from the world. (Avot 4:7)

- *Concerning the law and judicial matters.* The concept of justice and fairness of judges to everyone, no matter their economic or political status, is omnipresent in Pirkey Avot. Rabbi Shimon Ben Gamliel used to say, "The world stands on three things, on justice, truth and peace" (Avot 1:18).

Legal fairness is based on truth and impartiality and contributes to peace in the world. Fair judgment is made by a group of judges who deliberate and reach a fair verdict.

On this subject, another scholar, Rabbi Ishmael, implied in his teachings that the task of a judge is challenging. He also said that if a judge must render a verdict, he must hear the opinions of other judges because he could be wrong in his judgment if he did it alone. Rabbi Ishmael said, "Do not act as a judge alone because no one can judge alone expect the One [meaning God] and do not say, accept my opinion" (Avot 4:10).

- *Repent one day before you die.* It does not mean that you can get away with doing evil all or most of your life. What it means is that if you could not manage to do well all or most of your life, you might have a chance to ask for forgiveness just before you die.

  Rabbi Yaakov used to say on this topic, "It is better to have one hour of repentance and good deeds in this world than all the life of the world to come" (Avot 4:22).

- *Know where you came from.* Akabiah Ben Mahalalel helps us contemplate our point of origin and our last destination. We are here now, and we are made to die eventually. We are born from a fetid drop, and when we are buried, we are going to be eaten by worms and maggots. Therefore, one is to remain humble and do well in this life because, at the end, he is going to be accountable for his deeds. This outlook on life will help us stay away from evil as Akabiah said it,

  Look at three things and you can avoid sin. Know where you came from and where you are going and before whom you will be giving account. (Avot 3:1)

Incidentally, Akabiah had some legal disagreements with the majority of the court. He refused a high position as the head of the Sanhedrin because he stood his ground as he believed in himself. After his death, he was praised by none other than Rabbi Yehuda Hanassi (the Prince) who redacted the Mishnah.

- *When you eat or converse around a table, it is necessary to be spiritual.* Rabbi Hanina Ben Teradion and Rabbi Shimon Bar Yohai suggested that two or more people sitting around the table should be discussing words of the Torah.

In today's world, many people say a blessing or grace before and after a meal. Even as people conduct a business meeting, it is important to use wise quotes from the Bible or the Mishnah in order to make that meeting meaningful. Rabbi Shimon specified on this subject that "three [people] who eat at one table and say on it words of the Torah, it is as though they ate from the table of God" (Avot 3:4).

On the same subject, Rabbi Hanina said that when two people sit together and there are words of Torah between them, it is like "the spirit of God rests within them" (Avot 3:3).

- *Comparing wisdom to good deeds and fear of punishment.* Good deeds in the eyes of several scholars are preferable to wisdom. Wisdom can only be appreciated when it is accompanied with performing mitzvot (good deeds). The fear of God seems equal to fulfilling good deeds as Rabbi Haninah Ben Dosah puts it well:

> All those who put fear of sin before wisdom, wisdom prevails. All those who put wisdom before fear of sin, wisdom does not prevail . . . For that [person] whose good deeds exceed his wisdom, wisdom prevails. For that [person] whose wisdom exceeds his [good] deeds, wisdom does not prevail. (Avot 3:11–12)

- *Never embarrass your fellow person in public.* How authentic can this saying be? In the twenty-first century we try to be utterly diplomatic so people we criticize do not get embarrassed. Our sages knew that two millenniums ago. On this subject, Rabbi Eleazar the Modaiite said, "Whosoever desecrates sacred things, despises the festivals and embarrasses his fellow in public . . . does not have a share in the world to come" (Avot 3:15).

In the Talmudic world, where hundreds of ideas are debated in various academies, it is natural to have agreements and disagreements. We learned that certain scholars did not particularly agree with other scholars. What is more, there were incidents of animosity between scholars. A good example was the hatred against Elisha Ben Abuyah, who left the academy. We remember that Elisha Ben Abuyah, Rabbi Meir's teacher, turned to apostasy and neglected the laws of the Torah to the point of cooperating with the occupying Romans against rebellious Jews. Although Elisha was distanced from and even hated by most rabbis of his time, he was still appreciated by Rabbi Meir for his knowledge and wisdom. Even as he was considered wrong in the eyes of the academy and members of the community for becoming a heretic, he was still accepted by Rabbi Meir, his contemporary and old teacher.

- *Torah, the most valuable asset.* Rabbi Meir is among most luminaries who advocated the importance of the Torah as the most valuable asset a man or a woman can have. The Torah is not just for learning or studying, but it is also a guide to a good and meaningful life. The Torah also teaches peace and tolerance.

- Rabbi Meir advocated learning the Torah for its own sake and not as a demonstration of superiority or haughtiness. We learn from Rabbi Meir the following:

> Whoever is occupied with the Torah for its own sake achieves many things; what is more, the whole world is worthwhile for his sake alone. He is called a friend, a beloved. He loves God. He

loves people . . . He is dressed modestly and with fear [so as not to offend other people]. It conditions him to be righteous, pious, straightforward and faithful. It keeps him away from transgression . . . he becomes like a spring which keeps growing. He becomes humble and patient and forgives those who offend him. (Avot 6:1)

Rabbi Yohoshuah said on this subject that "you may not find a freer person than that [person] who is engaged in the Torah" (Avot 6: 2).

The sages of Avot implied that if one loves to study the Torah, even as he (or she) encounters discomfort, physically or financially, the study of the Torah can be done in any condition, as it is expressed in the following:

This is the way of the Torah: [if necessary] eat bread with salt and drink water by the quota; sleep on the ground and endure suffering while you are laboring in the Torah. If you do so, happy is you and good for you. Happy you in this world and it will be good for you in the world to come. Do not covet the table of kings, for your table is greater than theirs and your crown greater than theirs. (Avot 6:4–5)

Pirkey Avot summarizes the value of the Torah and compares it to priesthood and kingship. It says that the Torah has more degrees of importance than priesthood and even more than kingship. Priesthood is acquired by twenty-four degrees of importance, while kingship by thirty degrees. However, the Torah tops the above titles by having forty-eight degrees of importance including wisdom, humility, patience, love, moderation in socializing and achieving pleasure, justice, joy, fear of God, purity of the heart, unselfishness, and other qualities like the following:

Knowing one's place [recognizing where one comes from], being content with one's plot, being cautious while speaking, claiming no credit for oneself . . . avoiding fame, avoiding arrogance in one's knowledge . . . and whoever quotes a thing in the name of its author brings deliverance to the world . . . Torah is great, as it brings life to its doers in this world and in the world to come . . . it is a tree of life to those who hold on to it and those who support it shall be happy. (Avot 6:6–8)

The importance of the Torah in all its phases is implied in every chapter of Pirkey Avot. In modern times, the Hebrew Torah may be as valuable as other scriptures in other religions and cultures. All cultures which profess peace, tolerance, humility, love of God and people, unselfishness, justice and righteousness may be compared to the fine qualities included in the Torah.

- *Everything is predicted and watched from above.* We have no choice but to be honest, fair and do good deeds in this life. Rabbi Akiva is omnipresent in the Mishnah and Pirkey Avot. He adds that "all is predicted and yet freedom of choice is given; the world is judged in goodness and everything [a person does or does not do] is measured by the quantity if his deeds . . . and the judgment is a just judgment [for those who do good or evil]" (Avot 3:18–20).

- *Math and science are not contradictory to the Torah.* In fact, astronomy, astrology, and other sciences can be a great addition to the Torah. After all, God created heaven and earth, and it is not against the Halakhah to study the wonders of the universe.

  Rabbi Elazar Ben Hisma said, "The study of the stars and mathematics are an [important] addition to wisdom" (Avot 3:23).

- *Being part of the community and doing good things discretely.* Just as Rabbi Hillel encouraged everyone to be part of the community, Rabbi Tzadok said, "Do not separate yourself from the community . . . do not use [the Torah] as a crown to make yourself big." For more on Rabbi Tzadok, see chapter 14 ("Who is Who in Pirkey Avot").

  To the above, Yohanan the Shoemaker added that an assembly can only be good when it meets and acts for the sake of Heaven. He implied that the result would be justice and fairness, "Whereas one [an assembly] that is not [established] for the sake of Heaven will not endure" (Avot 4:14).

- *Concentrate on your prayer.* Rabbi Shimon, another Rabbi Shimon not mentioned often in this book, was one of the scholars who professed spending special time in prayer. He was especially particular about concentration and devotion while praying. In his time, he knew that some people prayed only for the sake of praying.

For Rabbi Shimon, prayer was a unique experience where a person is facing God and asking for mercy. He said, "Be careful when you recite the Shema [Hear, O Israel] and making the [silent] prayer [otherwise called the Amidah]. When you pray, do not make your prayer as a routine thing but [make it] as a plea for mercy and supplication before God. As it is said [in the book of Joel], 'For He is gracious and merciful, slow to anger and abounding in lovingkindness, and repenting upon evil'—do not be evil upon yourself" (Avot 2:18).

The above comment from Rabbi Shimon made many interpreters of the Mishnah think deeply. From Maimonides to Rashi, Bible and Mishnah scholars tried to find the real meaning behind Rabbi Shimon's warning.

It is without a doubt a profound statement as prayer is one of the most personal actions a man or a woman can do. The more sincere the person is the more the prayer can be called a real prayer. It is not lip service, and it is not considered a tax someone has to pay and forget about after it is paid.

When Rabbi Shimon asks us not to be mean to ourselves, he might mean several things like do not feel bad if your prayer is not perfect or make sure you are participating in a congregation so you do not have to pray alone.

Regarding the comment on God being merciful and repentant upon a tragedy caused to mankind or about to be caused, we found several instances when God regretted bringing the deluge on earth. When Moses pleaded before God to spare the Israelites from tragedy, God was merciful and forgiving. We also find, in the book of Jonah, that God spared the city of Nineveh after rescinding His decision to destroy the city when He found out that the people of Nineveh were ready to repent.

Prayer and the uttering of the Shema had a solemn meaning in the eyes of great rabbis like Rabbi Akiva who died at the hands of the Romans while reciting the Shema.

- *How is wisdom defined?* This is how anonymous sages describe the wise man in chapter 5 of

Pirkey Avot: The wise man does not challenge someone wiser than him nor does he interrupt people in the middle of the conversation. The wise man thinks before he answers. He does not rush to speak. He answers questions in the order they were posed. He admits the truth about what he heard and what he has not heard. The opposite qualities can be found in an uneducated person (per Avot 5:9).

- Ben Zoma, another scholar, tells us that a wise man is the one who can learn from every person (Avot 4:1).

- *On hospitality.* Hospitality is one of the highest qualities of righteousness. Hospitality is not just for friends but also for strangers. In everyday synagogue morning prayers, one of the commandments listed is hospitality to strangers.

One of the mitzvot (good deeds) established during Passover time is hospitality to anyone who wants to join the Seder ceremony and meal of Passover.

Yose Ben Yohanan said on this subject, "Let your house become open wide and let poor

people become members of your household"
(Avot 1:5).

- *On women.* Although women are not
profusely featured in the Avot book, there
is an entire order (seder) written on them in
the Mishnah and the Gemarah commentary.
Since women have an important duty to
raise children and maintain a household,
they have been exempt, according to the
Halakhah, from men's prayers (Amidah) and
from putting on the tefillin (phylacteries) and
the tsisit (talit).

However, in modern times, women have been
authorized in conservative congregations
to practically fulfill all the commandments
men do in the synagogue and within the
congregation.

Women are silent heroes in Pirkey Avot. For
example, Rabbi Akiva's wife was famous in
allowing her husband to be away for seven
years in order to study the Torah. She
encouraged him repeatedly to become an
erudite in the Torah while waiting for him

to come back as a proud scholar who was to make her a proud wife.

It is implied in the book of Avot that, in some ways, women hold an advantage as they have an attractive power over men. Therefore, the book of Avot forbids long talks with women. It does not blame women for talking to men, but it blames men for entertaining long talks with women and taking the risk of having their conversation with them lead to an immoral act.

On this subject, Yose Ben Yohanan, man of Jerusalem, said the following:

> And do not increase talk with a woman. This is said about one's own wife; all the more [this applies] to a friend's wife. From here the sages declared that whoever increases talk with a woman causes evil to himself and neglects the words of the Torah and in the end he will inherit Hell. (Avot 1:5)

In modern times, we have witnessed multiple accusations against prominent politicians, actors, and executives who betrayed their wives and were accused by the media for committing adultery, promiscuity, and sexual abuse.

- *Acquire a rabbi, a good teacher, and a good neighbor.* All the above is an attempt to enhance human relations between people either socially or intellectually.

Rabbi Yehoshua Ben Levi went to the extreme and taught that even if one learns only two words from a teacher or a rabbi, that teacher or rabbi deserves a special honor. Rabbi Yehoshua quoted the Bible when King David learned only two sayings from his adviser Ahitophel., "Whoever learns from his friend one chapter, or one legal version, or one sentence, or one saying or even one word; how much *more one must treat him with respect"* (Avot 6:3).

Rabbi Yehoshua Ben Perahiah and Nitai the Arbelite were among the pairs of rabbis who received the Torah from their predecessors

(Yosse Ben YoEzer and Yosse Ben Yohanan). The following is said about those two rabbis:

Yehoshua Ben Perahia said,

Get yourself a rabbi, and acquire a friend and judge every one within the benefit of the doubt. Nitai the Arbelite said: keep away from a bad neighbor and do not associate with the wicked person and do not despair from divine calamities. (Avot 1:7)

The above profound statement about calamities or retribution could have been said in regard to Alexander Yanai (103 BCE–76 BCE) who persecuted the Pharisees amid a civil war. He was a Sadducee himself. While he observed some Torah rules like marrying his dead brother's wife, he did not respect the temple rituals, and he had thousands of Pharisees executed because they did not agree with the way he performed the rituals. He certainly could not be compared to the great Shammai or Hillel the Elder who never conducted wars between themselves but insisted instead on intellectual and biblical debates. Alexander, of the Hasmonean Dynasty, could not be compared to his Hasmonean ancestor, Mathathias the Priest and Judah the Maccabee, his son, who liberated the temple from the Greeks (160 BCE). The violence caused by Alexander prompted Yehoshuah Ben Perahiah to flee to Egypt.

- *Who is rich?* The book of Avot invokes the psalms of David and the proverbs of King Solomon by concluding that the rich man is the one who is happy with what he has. In other words, the man who is happy with his plot does not envy richer people than him is a content man (per Avot 4:1).

We have seen earlier that the Talmudic scholars considered a rich man to be a man who is versed in the Torah. A person who is occupied with observing the commandments of the Torah in this world is spiritually rich in his own right. His wisdom and acceptance of God allows him to earn a rich future in the world to come.

The sages suggest that people should be happy with what they earn as a result of their hard work.

- *On respect and human relations.* Respect between two people or more is a theme frequently repeated in the book of Avot. In chapter 4, we find that respect is reciprocal between people as Ben Zoma said, "Who should be the person to be respected [and the answer is] it is the person who respects humankind" (Avot 4:1).

Ben Zoma, concerning respect to others, credits the book of Samuel in the Bible by repeating this, "For, those who respect me I shall respect and those who despise me shall be shamed" (1 Samuel 2:30).

In addition, Pirkey Avot advises us to be courteous to everyone. This implies that all people should be greeted well, including those people with a bad temper or bad manners. This also implies that everyone deserves the benefit of the doubt, especially when someone does not know anything about another person.

Three of the five disciples of Rabbi Yohanan Ben Zakkai (spoken about above) are quoted as saying different things on this subject, as follows. Rabbi Eliezer, the first disciple, said the following:

> The honor of your friend should be as dear as your own and do not be easy to anger. (Avot 2:15)

Rabbi Yehoshua, the second disciple, said the following:

> An evil eye, the evil impulse and hatred of mankind drive a person out of this world. (Avot 2:16)

The third disciple, Rabbi Yose, said the following:

> Let the possessions of your fellow person be as dear as your own. (Avot 2:17)

We recall that Rabbi Elazar Ben Arach, the fifth disciple, said that a good heart is the best quality in a person. Rabbi Yohanan Ben Zakkai found that a good heart included all the best qualities in a person. On this subject, another scholar, Rabbi Matya Ben Harash, said, "Be first to greet everyone" (Avot 4:20).

- *Honor and respect extend to students as well.* Rabbi Elazar Ben Shamua, a student of Rabbi Akiba and a teacher of Rabbi Yehuda Hanassi, was a very respected scholar. Speaking about honor in the field of education, he said:

> The honor of your student should be as precious as your own and the honor of your colleague should be as the honor of your teacher and the honor of your teacher should be equal to the fear of Heaven. (Avot 4:15)

We have seen here how respect and honor extend from a simple person to a student and to a teacher. The seriousness attributed to a fellow student and to a teacher and a rabbi is equivalent to respecting and honoring God Himself.

- *Prayers can be accepted by God no matter how many people pray.* Even as it preferable for a person to join a congregation of ten people or more in order to make a prayer, some sages send us words of comfort in assuring us that God can hear a prayer even if just one person is involved.

Rabbi Hanina Ben Teradion, another passionate scholar, lived in the Holy Land after the rebellion of Bar Kochbah (135 CE). He taught the Torah despite the prohibition by the occupying Romans to discontinue its teaching in the Holy Land. He was arrested and burned to death as a punishment. Nevertheless, his name is mentioned in Yom Kippur as one of the ten martyrs who died for no other reason than the fact that he loved God and the Torah.

According to Rabbi Hanina, divine presence rests within two people or even one person. As it said,

> When two people sit together and words of Torah are between them, the Shekhinah [the divine spirit] rests between them . . . [and] how do we know, that even

if one person sits and occupies himself with the Torah, that the Almighty gives him a reward? As it is said [in Lamentations 3:28], let him sit alone and [pray] quietly, for [the Lord] will have a reward for him. (Avot 3:3)

Rabbi Halaphtah Ben Dosah, a contemporary of Rabbi Akiva, also touched on the subject of prayer by one or more people. Rabbi Halaphtah quotes from the Bible that whether it is ten people or even one person praying, the divine presence is always there to reward the praying person or persons. As it said by him,

And how do we know, that even if it is one person [praying]. As it is said [in Exodus] in every place when my name is mentioned I will come to you and bless you. (Avot 3:7)

- *This world is a bridge to the world to come.* It is imperative to perform as many good deeds as possible in this life so one can be welcome in the world to come. Most sages in Pirkey Avot imply that the afterlife is about to come for those who do well in this world.

Rabbi Yaakov is more explicit and warns us to prepare ourselves for the world to come so we have a chance to enjoy an afterlife.

Rabbi Yaakov said, "This world is a hallway before the world to come. Prepare yourself in that hallway so you can enter the Traklin [the banquet hall of the afterlife]" (Avot 4:21).

- *Do not desecrate God's name in secret.* It is already forbidden to profane God's name in public. One who desecrates the name of Heaven either inadvertently or deliberately ends up being known to the public and is punished accordingly. As we learn in this Mishnah, nothing a person does is hidden forever. At the end, the truth prevails. People who pretend to pray and are outwardly pious can be caught for their hypocrisy. To this Rabbi Yohanan Ben Berukah, a student of Rabbi Yehoshua, said,

"Whoever profanes the name of Heaven secretly, is prone to being punished in public; whether it [the profanation] is done inadvertently or willfully" (Avot 4:5).

- *Try not to forget what you learned because knowledge of laws demands responsibility.* Rabbi Yehuda was a disciple of Rabbi Akiva and one of the teachers of Yehuda Hanassi (the Prince). Emphasis is made here to find no excuses for forgetting or ignoring any part of the law when one teaches or renders justice. Forgetting or ignoring any halakhic law is considered extremely irresponsible. To this Rabbi Yehuda said,

  > Be careful in the [halakhic Talmud], because error in teaching [or judging] can amount to intentional sin. (Avot 4:16)

- *One hour of repentance in this life can be comparable to the life in the coming world.* In contrast, one hour of bliss in the world to come is better than the entire duration of life in this world. This opinion by Rabbi Jacob can be debated between humans and between scholars. Several commentators found this statement paradoxical. Nevertheless, the first part of the sentence seems important as it is necessary to repent in this world we know and do good deeds in order to prepare us for the world to come that we do not know. Nevertheless, no one can be admitted to the world to come without earning merits in this world.

He [Rabbi Yaakov] used to say, "Better is one hour of repentance and good deeds in this world than all the life of the world to come. [In addition] better is one hour of bliss in the world to come than all the life in this world" (Avot 4:22).

- *"Do not pacify your fellow person in a moment of anger."* These are words of wisdom from Rabbi Shimon Ben Eleazar who was a student of Rabbi Meir and a colleague of Rabbi Yehuda Hanassi. An angry person could become angrier when people try to speak to him in the moment of his anger and while he has not regained his cool state of mind. It is best to wait for your friend to calm down. Furthermore,

Rabbi Shimon Ben Eleazar advised not to console a friend but to remain silent in the hour that his dead (relative) lies before him. When a friend or a relative is overwhelmed with emotion, it is best to keep a low profile as a gesture of respect and understanding. It is also better to console a friend after the burial of his loved one. The rabbi also advised us not to question a friend in the moment of his vow. One person making a pledge can be embarrassed if someone else interferes with him while making that pledge. Finally, Rabbi Shimon asks us to keep away from a friend who had his moment of disgrace. This demonstrates understanding and compassion for a friend who is in his moment of demise. Silence, not words, would help a friend recover from his embarrassment.

Those words of wisdom contain three situations when a friend or associate is in the middle of something. All have in common that special timing when one friend should choose to remain silent and not crowd another friend.

Rabbi Shimon Ben Eleazar said,

"Do no pacify your friend in his moment of anger and do no console him in the hour that his dead [relative] lies before him and do not question him in the moment of his vow and do not try to visit him in his hour of disgrace" (Avot 4:23).

- *Do not rejoice when your enemy falls, loses, or is beaten.* Jewish tradition teaches that all people on earth are children of God, including your enemy. It is better to remain sober and avoid any celebration when your enemy has lost his battles. This practice is still observed in today's Passover Seders when we pour ten drops of wine on a plate (symbolizing the ten plagues inflicted over Egypt), thus sympathizing with the historic Egyptians armies and soldiers who sank into the Red Sea when they pursued the freed Israelites. That advice is from Samuel the Young who said, "Do not rejoice when your enemy falls and when he stumbles do not your let your heart be glad lest the Lord see it and become displeased, [thus] turning his anger from him to you" (Avot 4:24).

- *Do not look at objects from the outside and judge them as they appear.* Rabbi Meir was one of the most scholarly leaders in his time and he taught us that maxim, which can be found in other cultures. We should never underestimate a person by his or her appearance. We need to realize that that person who appears plain on the outside could turn out to be a genius.

- *Jealousy, envy, and haughtiness drive a person out this world* (Avot 4:28). Those words are from Rabbi Elazar Hakappar, who warns us to remain humble and not seek too much honor or fame. Some people deserve to be respected for their actions. That is normal. However, some people lack humility and seek to be first in line in being recognized by the public. That is not acceptable.

- *We are born to live and die and give account for our deeds.* These are more words from Rabbi Eleazar Hakappar who says that without our agreement, we are born, we die, and we are to be judged at the end of days, whether we like it or not. Rabbi Eleazar said further, "Those who are born are destined to die and the dead are for [the after] life; and the living for judgment . . . He is the judge . . . in whose presence there is no obliquity and no forgetfulness and no favoritism and no bribe taking and know that everything is accounted for" (Avot 4:29).

- *Anonymous sayings in Pirkey Avot.* In chapter 5 we learn that there were ten generations from Adam to Noah. Ten generations form Noah to Patriarch Abraham. Abraham went through ten trials before God. Ten miracles occurred in Egypt before the Israelites were freed. Ten miracles occurred at the Red Sea. Ten plagues were inflicted on Egypt. Ten times the Israelites challenged the Word of God. Ten miracles occurred in the temple (including the fact that rain never put out the fire in the altar, the wind never blew away the smoke coming from the altar, and there was enough room for every Israelite in Jerusalem despite the fact that Jerusalem could not possibly have accommodated the multitude of people who showed up for the pilgrimages). It is also said in that chapter that ten things were created on Sabbath eve, including the rainbow of Noah, the manna of the desert, and the tablets of the Ten Commandments (based on Avot 5:5–8).

- *Predictions announced in Chapter 5.* As mentioned above, not bringing the tithe to the temple is a serious transgression. When a tithe is not accurate and even when some people bring the accurate tithe and some other people bring less than the right measure, it is considered a transgression for all. The punishment is grave: famine for some and plenty for others (Avot 5:10). The contribution of the challah (special bread, a dough-cake for the priest and the poor) by women was also a serious commandment to follow. Failure to fulfill that mitzvah could lead to fatal famine (Avot 5:10). The original commandment of the bread contribution is mentioned in the book of Numbers (15:20). Other predictions of calamities (such as pestilence and the sword) are announced for lack of observing the sabbatical year for the land and for perversion of justice. The commandment of the sabbatical year for the land is mentioned in the book of Leviticus

25:3–6. Another prediction is the arrival of the wild beast for desecrating the name of God. Exile from the land will take place for the pursuit of idolatry, for lewdness, and for bloodshed. Pestilence increases for neglecting to give the tithe for the poor and the deprived and for the violation of the seventh year sabbatical of the land (Avot 5:11–13). The commandment about helping the poor and the stranger in the land was already cited in the book of Deuteronomy 24–19.

- Could those warnings have influenced the way we operate today in the twenty-first century? Perhaps. We know that generosity throughout the world is present in helping countries in distress. Following tsunamis and earthquakes abroad and hurricanes here in the United States, we learn about generous people who extend their hands and help in the relief effort with generous contributions. The tithe in biblical times can be compared to paying taxes in our time. Whereas it is illegal to cheat on taxes, it was forbidden then to cheat on tithes.

- *What is mine is yours and what is yours is yours is pious (Avot 5:14).* A pious man acts this way. The opposite is evil, meaning a wicked man claims that his fellow's property belongs to him while his own property remains his. This person wants all for himself without sharing or even swapping property with someone else. Pirkey Avot also speaks about the average person who says, "Mine is mine and yours is yours." That is considered fair with an exception. The exception is that, according to scriptures, a portion of a person's wealth is to be shared with the poor people. "Mine is yours and yours is mine" is considered ignorant by Pirkey Avot because neither one of those two people know what the other fellow has. If they already knew, it will be unjust to swap unequal properties between two people unless they had a mutual agreement to do so. This idea of what belongs to who leads us to the biblical commandment that all property belongs to God and the best way to deal with property and possessions is to share them with the poor and the priests of the temple.

Chapter Sixteen

The Mishnaic Period and the Christian Connection

Jesus and the Early Christian Jews in the Talmudic Era

The early Christian Jews who accepted Christianity and who followed Jesus and his apostles before and immediately after his death represented a combination of God-fearing religious and pious people and some other "uneducated, superstitious, and fanatical people," as Heschel cites in a quote from Geiger's book *Das Judentum.*

We must say first that the original people who followed Jesus were from the north of the Holy Land, in Samaria. At the time the Talmud and the Mishnah were being studied, formed, and redacted (between 200 BCE and 300 CE), the people of the Holy Land were divided into north and south. In the north, the Samaritans worshiped at Mount Gerizim, while the Jews in the middle and south of the Holy Land observed their yearly or biyearly pilgrimage to Jerusalem in the south.

Talmudic interpreters report that the Samaritans may have been the descendants of the northern Israel Kingdom, which severed ties with the kingdom of Judah in the south.

Consequently, Jesus has been described as follows:

> He was a Jew, a Pharisean Jew with Galilean coloring, man who shared the hopes of his time and who believed that these hopes were fulfilled in him. He did not utter a new thought, nor did he break down the barriers of nationality. He did not abolish any part of Judaism; he was a Pharisee who walked in the way of Hillel . . . [as he] proclaimed that, ". . . not the least title should be taken from the Law; the Pharisees sit in Moses' seat, and what they say you should observe and obey."

As we further look into the ascetic background of Jesus, we learn that it was not until the twentieth century, in 1947, that the Dead Sea Scrolls were discovered. Those scrolls revealed many details on the Essenes society of the land of Israel.

The Dead Sea Scrolls described, among other things, the ascetic and separatist way of life of the Essenes and their leaving the city of Jerusalem for the desert where the ruins of Qumran (Khirbet Qumran) exist today in the proximity of the Dead Sea.

Interestingly, the Dead Sea Scrolls speak of the decision of a minority of Jews who chose to live in the arid desert of the Holy Land in order to escape the harshness of the Roman occupation of the land of Israel and the hypocrisy of the existing governor of the land: Herod and his sons.

The Essenes made it clear that they also resented the way the Holy Temple of Jerusalem had been administered and run by the priests of the time, covering an estimated one hundred years preceding and succeeding the advent of Jesus.

The language used about the way of life of the Essenes seems similar to the language used by Jesus when he addressed the authorities of the Holy Temple of Jerusalem.

Dr. Hugh J. Schonfield is an important translator of the New Testament and author of *Secrets of the Dead Sea Scrolls.* In his book *The Passover Plot: A New Interpretation of the Life and Death of Jesus,* it is said about the leaders of the council of the Essenes who regarded themselves as doing an act of atoning for the whole Jewish community of the Holy Land that

> they shall preserve the Faith in the land with steadfastness and meekness, and shall atone for sin by the practice of justice and by suffering the sorrows of affliction . . . And they shall be an agreeable offering, atoning for the land and determining the judgment of wickedness, and there shall be no more iniquity.

The Dead Sea Scrolls offered voluminous and copious data about the Bible, including the Pentateuch, which mostly covers the laws of Moses. They also covered the biblical prophets, namely Isaiah. Various interpretations of the Bible were included in those important scrolls.

Allusions to the end of days are one of the basic ideas of the Essenes expressed on those precious writings. Documents titled *War of the Sons of Light against the Sons of Darkness* explain how those who truly follow the laws of Moses as prescribed by God can be considered the sons of light as opposed to those who misinterpret the laws of the Bible and the arrival of a redeeming prophet.

The hopes for the arrival of a godly person in the likeliness and the caliber of Moses the prophet are expressed throughout various texts of the scrolls. Just as some Judeans hoped for the coming of another Moses, the early Christians who were devout Jews were hoping for the coming of a Messiah such as Jesus.

From so many scholars, writers, and researchers on early Christianity history, we chose this quote from Dr. Schonfield about the formation of early Christianity and the advent of Jesus:

> The motives of Jesus must be sought in the land where he was born and the times in which he lived. On his own showing, he was not sent except for the lost sheep of the house of Israel.

They were oppressed. Their country was controlled by a powerful heathen people, governed by its officials and their representatives. They suffered. They were in dread. They sinned and were wretched, angry, and anxious. Yet upon their redemption, there waited the peace and happiness of the whole world, which should arise from Israel's return to the Lord, when the worship of One God and Father would be extended to all the children of men. The Scribes instructed in the Kingdom of God had made known that the Last Times of the old order had come, that the Messiah would speedily be revealed as the instrument of the great change, the Regeneration . . . The Shepherd himself would be required to give his life for the sheep. All this Jesus saw and believed, and found in his heart a great love and compassion for his people.

What is important to know is that Jesus's message was not only directed toward his Israelite brethren but toward humanity as a whole. Jesus believed with all his heart that he was the real Messiah, the redeemer of Israel as well as the whole humanity.

Jesus and Pikey Avot (The Wisdom of the Fathers)

As the language found in the New Testament testifies, Jesus himself, in his preaching and teaching, seemed to be familiar with Pirkey Avot (even before its completion). Subjects such as moral conduct, humility, deprivation, dealing with the authorities, how to pray without being a fanatic, and how you should care about your fellow man as you would care about yourself, are all subjects found in Pirkey Avot.

Jesus, who knew the Torah and the Book of Prophets, could quote verbatim many passages from those books in order to justify the prophecy of his mission to become the redeemer of Israel and humanity. Simultaneously, we could detect some passages in the New Testament reminding us of the language of Pirkey Avot, a book widely read and revered by the Jewish and non-Jewish faithful to the day.

Maxims like "You should love your fellow person as you love yourself" is a maxim implicated by Jesus on many occasions throughout the New Testament. It has been found earlier in the Pentateuch, and later on, it had been credited to Hillel the Sage and Rabbi Akiva.

"Who is [considered] wise?" Pirkey Avot asks. "He who learns from every human being." This quote had been attributed to Simon Ben Zoma, a contributor to Pirkey Avot. It has also been found in the book of Psalms chapter 119, saying, "I have gained wisdom from all my instructors (u-mikkol Melamedai Hiskalti).

'Who is rich? That person who is content with his plot [who is happy with what he (she) has]." That message of modesty and simplicity, found in Pirkey Avot, was repeatedly sent by Jesus to his disciples and to plain folks in the Holy Land.

"Who is mighty? This who controls his emotions." This maxim is also found in Pirkey Avot, and it had already been mentioned in the book of Proverbs. It can be said that Jesus followed this maxim when he carefully planned his arrival at the temple without disclosing any details, even to his apostles. His triumphal arrival to Jerusalem, according to the New Testament and scholarly reviews, showed that

Jesus was able to control himself and not divulge any of his revelations until the time was right.

Jesus seemed to have exercised control of himself, based on the quote of the biblical Proverbs he knew so well and which said, "One who is slow to anger is preferred to one who is [physically] strong, and one who controls his emotions [is preferred] to one who captures a city" (Proverbs 16:32).

The above quotes, and many more to be counted, are just an example of the Pharisaic quotes of the book of the Wisdom the Fathers (Avot), which have been incorporated by Jews into their daily prayers. They have also been adopted by Christian scholars and Christian speakers who wanted to demonstrate the ancient Hebrew wisdom and the language in which Jesus expressed himself when he addressed the crowds of his followers.

It is without a doubt that the Pentateuch, the Book of the Prophets, the biblical writings, and the book of Pirkey Avot, had a vivid influence on the language and the feeling of Jesus when he addressed the early Christians throughout the Holy Land in his attempt to rectify society in the land of Israel and, eventually, the world society in general.

Christian-Christian and Christian-Jewish Debate

Since the establishment of Christianity there has been a recurring gross misunderstanding between Christians and Christians, between Christians and non-Christians, and finally, between Christians and Jews. Christians became more and more numerous after the conversion of pagan conquerors and Hellenistic forces blended with the early Christianity, originally inspired by the Jewish wisdom of Jesus and his disciples.

Jesus revered the laws of the Torah and the true meanings behind the commandments of God in the Pentateuch. He was the original and rare rabbi of his generation who professed love and peace between friends and enemies. His apostles, whether or not they carried Jesus's message to the letter, brought the idea of monotheism to the world and to humanity. That message was originally inspired by the laws of Moses, which Jesus himself cherished, observed, and revered.

A domino effect occurred in the manner of interpreting the early instructions of the Torah in which Jesus believed and wanted his disciples and apostles to believe in.

According to many historians, the changes that occurred in Christianity began with Paul.

More apostles who spoke for Jesus had in some ways, consistent tales about the marvels of Jesus and his extraordinary impact on the Jews of Galilee and other Jews from the south of the Holy Land who adhered to his teachings. One who studies the New Testament can find similarities as well as contradictions in the tales of the apostles and the Messianic message handed down by Jesus himself.

The early message of Christianity was a message of love and brotherhood. It was a message of religious reform of the existing status quo. It was not intended to create a new religion. The evolution of Christianity throughout history and the various interpretations and amendments made to it made Christianity a religion that can have various ways of worship. It made Christianity a religion where man can change the original words of the scriptures, the Word of God, as perceived by Jesus, according to the Christian tradition.

Those biblical words and commandments were adapted and adjusted by the new rulers of Christianity throughout history.

It is, therefore, understandable now that many Christians believe that the Old Testament is an archaic document, which was to be replaced by a new document called the New Testament. Christian believers and scholars, led by Jesus himself, kept referring to and quoting the Old Testament and the Book of Prophets (especially the book of Isaiah) in order to justify the prophecy of Jesus and the establishment of a new world order on earth.

The question remains though, If the Old Testament is that archaic and irrelevant in the eyes of some Christians, why then do they use it and quote it in order to justify the existence and the message of Jesus?

In conclusion, in Geiger's opinion, Jesus was first a Jew, and a pious Jew, who wanted to change the social and religious status quo in the Holy Land and, eventually, in the world. He did that with the mental powers he had, which were borrowed from his Jewish, Pharisee, and Essenes background, mixed with the traditional divine power he possessed.

Christianity of today is not necessarily what Jesus was talking about in order to amend the world he was born in. Jesus had no idea there would be another religion after his death. Christianity is a mixture of ideas, using the Old and New Testament and the other cultures, which dominated European lands and blended with them by accepting Christ as their savior.

Chapter Seventeen

Influence of Mishnaic Sages on Today's Jewish Tradition and Rituals

If we could make a short statement on several rabbis and sages who shaped the Jewish rituals as observed today in most synagogues, temples, and other houses of worship, we would come out with the following findings:

* Akiba (Akiva). His name dominates the Talmud. He is also mentioned on Yom Kippur, as a part of the ritual service, as one of the ten martyrs murdered by the occupying Romans for promoting the Torah. His main saying was "love your neighbor as yourself". This is a saying frequently used in every culture. (For more sayings of Rabbi Akiva, see chapters 14 and 15.)

* Antigonus, Man of Socho. He received the Torah from Simon the Just (see above). His Greek name

indicates that the Jewish life in the Holy Land was under Greek influence.

* Aquila. He translated the Bible from Hebrew to Greek. This is another indication of Greek influence in the Holy Land (he was a non-Jew who was converted to Judaism).

* Ashi. He was the first editor of the Babylonian Talmud, and he reestablished the academy of Surah.

* Ravina. He completed the work of Ashi in the year 500. Ravina is also known to have initiated the breaking of a glass during a wedding ceremony, a tradition still followed today. The breaking of a glass, while celebrating, is also is a symbol of mourning for the destruction of the Jerusalem temple and an expression of a wish to prevent possible disasters after a wedding.

* Ben Bag Bag. He is known for urging his people to delve into the Torah without stop. He said, "Delve in it and continue to delve in it."

* Ben Bavah. He was one of the ten martyrs killed by the Romans for promoting the Torah. While

waiting for his death, he ordained five rabbis including Rabbi Akiva and Rabbi Meir.

* Rabbi Eleazar Ben Arach. His teacher, Rabbi Yohanan Ben Zakkai, described his wisdom as "a flowing spring."

* Ben Zoma. He introduced the tradition of making a one-time blessing over the bread before a meal without having to make multiple blessings over the other food items.

* Eleazar Ben Azariah. He was known to have said that the Bible speaks in the language of humans and that good deeds surpass wisdom.

* Eleazar Ben Yose. He stated that repentance brings forgiveness. A person may repent up to three times but no more. Repentance is a spiritual force that brings most Jews together during the high holidays (Rosh Hashanah and Yom Kippur).

* Eleazar Ben Yehuda of Bartuta. His main concern was about giving to the poor. The tradition of generosity continues all over the world in synagogues and churches.

* Eleazar Ben Mattai. He was one of the four scholars who understood seventy languages.

* Eleazar Ben Pedat. He taught that one should set the table for the Sabbath even if one is not hungry and even if he has to consume a small amount of food, as small as the size of an olive.

* Eleazar Ben Shamua. According to him, an accomplished scholar should master the Midrash, the Aggadah (legend), and the Tosephta (the additional sources to the Talmud). These three things are often quoted by rabbis in their sermons to the congregation.

* Eleazar Hakappar. He is known for saying, "Jealousy, lust, and pursuit of fame remove a man from this world."

* Eleazar of Moddin. His famous saying was, "Do not embarrass your fellow person in public." This is universal advice to all humanity. Rabbi Eleazar was also the uncle of Bar Kokhbah.

* Eleazar Ben Hyrkanus. He was known in Pirkey Avot as "a cemented well which does not lose a drop" because he had a super memory. He was one of the two students of Yohanan Ben Zakkai who

carried their teacher for safety out of Jerusalem in order to meet Vespasian and obtain permission to found an academy in Yavneh.

* Elisha Ben Abuyah. Originally a great Jewish scholar, he turned heretic in the eyes of his contemporaries but was admired by his student Rabbi Meir.

* Rabban Gamaliel I. He was the grandson of Hillel and a well-respected head of the Sanhedrin. He is known, according to the New Testament, to be the teacher of Paul. He initiated the well-known tradition in Jewish burial to be in linen shrouds rather than in expensive cloths.

* Gamliel II. As a head of the Sanhedrin, he established the House of Hillel to be the final authority on Judaism after a peaceful unification with the House of Shammai. He was also behind the establishment of the blessings of the Amidah (the silent prayer said three times daily in the Jewish rituals).

* Gamliel III. He is known for urging his people to combine the study of the Torah with an occupation.

He also warned us to beware of the authorities. The above qualities are well observed today.

* Gamliel V. He helped to complete the Jewish calendar.

* Gamliel VI. He was the last patriarch of the House of Hillel. His authority as the head of the Sanhedrin was terminated by the Roman regime in the year 415 CE. Fortunately, the Jewish tradition was preserved in the Diaspora.

* Halafta. He established proper procedures for blowing the shofar. The Shofar is blown in Rosh Hashanah and at the end of Yom Kippur.

* Halafta Ben Dosa. He excelled in explaining and proving through quotes in the scriptures that whether one person or ten people or more pray to God, divine presence resides within them. Observing people may pray alone at home when they are unable to attend congregation services.

* Hannan Bar Abba. He established that the answer "Amen" to a prayer should be said in a lower tone of voice than the prayer itself. This response is uttered several times each in daily prayers.

* Hananiah Ben Akashia. He is quoted at the end of every chapter of Pirkey Avot where he said that all the people of Israel have a share in the world to come. Mishnah commentators say that the words of Hananiah mean that God gave the Israelites, out of his love for Israel, many laws to follow. This was contradictory to the Pauline view that God gave laws to the Israelites in order to increase their sins and have them pray for forgiveness. Rabbi Hananiah's view was cherished by the redactors of the Mishnah and Pirkey Avot.

* Hanania Ben Hakina. He is also one the ten martyrs mentioned in Yom Kippur during the martyrology service (a special service done in Yom Kippur memorializing those rabbis who died for resisting the Roman conquerors who forbade the study of the Torah in the Holy Land). He was a colleague of Rabbi Akiba. Both names are among the 10 names mentioned on Yom Kippur during the martyrology service.

* Hanania Ben Teradion. He was one of the martyrs as well. During the service memorializing his name, it is said that he died bravely while being burned alive and while wrapped with Torah scrolls. He is known to have said to his students that while the

scrolls were burning with him, the holy letters of the scrolls were flying off the fire.

* Hanina Bar Hama. He is known in Jewish tradition to have reinforced the thought that all that happens to people is predicted by heaven. Yet people have the choice to do well or to commit evil. As he put it, "Everything is in the hand of Heaven except the fear of God." He is also behind the tradition of wearing special garments on the Sabbath day and holidays.

In today's religions worldwide, most congregants dress properly for worship and save their best garments for special days and holidays.

* Hanina Ben Dosa. Like other sages, he emphasized that doing good deeds is more important than wisdom. Performing good deeds is an important part of Jewish tradition and all religious traditions worldwide.

* Hanina Segan Hakohanin (second to the high priest).He was famous in saying, "Pray for the welfare of the government." This is a Jewish tradition that is found in the book of Jeremiah and that was preserved since the Roman occupation

of the Holy Land. In synagogues worldwide, the congregants pray for the existing government, usually of Mondays, Thursdays and on the Sabbath and holidays when the Torah is read.

* Hillel. Hillel the Great is among the most quoted sages in the Jewish tradition. He is known to be the father of Halakhah (legal matters compatible with the Torah) as approved by all or most branches of Judaism. Among his famous sayings we quote, "Do not say, when I am free I shall study, perhaps you may not [ever] be free." His maxim "Do not separate yourself from the community' has a remarkable impact on people today who are part of a congregation or church leaders who advance the agendas in helping the poor and the needy. Hillel the Great made many more wise statements, which are listed above under Pikey Avot (The Wisdom of the Fathers).

* Hillel II. He continued the tradition of the House of Hillel. He also established and corrected the existing Jewish calendar to make it a permanent calendar. The new calendar became useful for Jews in the Holy Land as well as for the Jews in the Diaspora.

* Hisda. Among many traditions he established, the one observed today on the day before Passover is using a candle to search for leavened bread designed to be burned the morning before Passover Eve.

* Hya Bar Abba. He instilled the tradition to make a blessing over wine during the havdalah service (on Saturday night at the conclusion of the Sabbath). He is also known for saying that the Sabbath is a day of pure enjoyment (a tradition well-preserved).

* Hya Bar Ami. Inspired by Psalm 128, he excelled in encouraging people to live from their work rather than being handed charities even if they study the Torah. Although it is a tradition in all synagogues, churches, and mosques to give charity, it is also preferable that all people who need to be supported find a paying job.

* Rav Huna. He was behind the timing of searching for the hametz (meaning what was the right time for observant Jews to look for the unleavened bread to be burned on the morning before Passover Eve). He also advocated generosity toward others and proper behavior in the synagogue. Traditionally, in modern times, all the unleavened food is usually

disposed of or burned between the hours of 10 am and 12 Pm, the morning before the Passover holiday.

* Imma Shalom. She was a highly learned and intellectual woman. She was admired by her husband, Rabbi Eliezer Ben Hyrkanus, and her brother, Rabbi Gamliel II. Most women today can be proud of her as she is represented in the Talmud as an equal to others for her wisdom.

* Issac Bar Nappahah (Isaac the Blacksmith). He was considered one of the masters of the Aggadah (legend), thus demonstrating the importance of the Torah throughout legends and stories. His attitude to poor people was not just about giving money but encouragement and good counseling.

This tradition is observed today in all or most nonprofit institutions whose leaders try to help needy people with dignity and compassion.

* Ishmael Ben Elisha. Besides his expert halachic (legal) knowledge, he was one of the rabbis who advocated using proper words to describe delicate situations, such as going to the restroom or having

an intimate relationship with a woman. This is appropriate in today's world.

* Jonathan Ben Eleazar. As a head of the Academy of Sephoris, he was so serious about how a judge should be impartial that if he were not fair in his judgment, he would deserve hell (Gehinom). He also stressed the importance of education. He said if a teacher or a learned man taught a simple and uneducated person, also called an am haaretz, "God will annul all decrees against him." In modern times, all institutions, religious or not, strive to promote justice and education.

* Yose Ben Yehuda. His aggadic (his way of saying legends) genius inspired Shalom Aleichem, a famous Yiddish writer of the nineteenth century and the author of *Tevye (Tuvia) the Milkman,* on which a movie was created: *Fiddler on the Roof.* That best-selling book became a worldwide masterpiece, which also turned into a Hollywood prizewinning movie and a lasting Broadway show.

* Yehoshua Ben Gamla. A wealthy high priest of the first century, he was the first to establish and help fund elementary schools in the land of Israel. Until then, most children studied at home. We

know that today's religious institutions worldwide have established religious elementary and Sunday schools for children and adults in order to pursue their religious education.

* Yehoshua Ben Hananiah and Eliezer Ben Hyrcanus. They were considered the two scholars who indirectly saved the Hebrew tradition after the destruction of the second temple. They were students of Rabbi Yohanan Ben Zakkai. They both managed to transport their master, in a coffin, out of the besieged Jerusalem. If it were not for them, Yohanan Ben Zakkai would have lost his opportunity to open a new academy in Yabneh, and thus, it might have seriously damaged the continuity of the study of the Torah. Both rabbis were among the zuggot (pairs of scholars) who received the Torah and its interpretation from their predecessors. Interestingly, both scholars seem to represent the friendly and peaceful divide existing today between orthodox and conservative (more liberal) Jews. Joshua Ben Hananiah was of the House of Hillel (more flexible and practical), while Eliezer Ben Hyrcanus was of the House of Shammai (who stuck to the Torah rules as they were prescribed). In the end, as indicated earlier,

the House of Hillel prevailed because it won thanks to the majority rule established by all rabbis in cases of most judicial and religious matters.

* Joshua Ben Perahiah and Nitai the Arbelite (Haarbeli). Both were leading scholars who were part of the zuggot (pairs). Joshua was a nassi (president of the Sanhedrin), and Nitai was head of court (av bet din). As their previous zuggot, Ben Perahiah, was of the House of Hillel, while Nitai was of the House of Shammai, both supported education, faith, and justice. This is something houses of worship worldwide strive at achieving today.

* Yehuda Ben Illai. He was a second-century scholar who made passionate statements about the importance of charity. He claimed that "charity brings redemption closer". Giving charity is a most important act of Judaism and of most religions.

* Yehuda II. He was another precursor of elementary school education. He also was the grandson of Yehudah Hanassi.

* Yehudah Ben Batra. Most Jewish people in mourning follow the tradition instilled by Yehuda

Ben Batra by making a single tear in one's garment to demonstrate sadness over the passing of a relative or a friend.

* Yehudah Ben Tabbai and Shimon Ben Shetah. They were another pair of scholars (zuggot) who received the tradition from their predecessors. They were both judges who disagreed about the death penalty. While Shimon Ben Shetah enforced the death penalty even if the defendant turned out to be innocent, Yehudah Ben Tabbai did not rush to condemn the defendant, although he once allowed the death penalty of an innocent person. Shimon Ben Shetah concluded after he allowed the death of an accused defendant (in this case, it was his own son) that the witnesses must be carefully and meticulously examined and cross-examined in order to prevent baseless bloodshed. Shimon Ben Shetah was also behind the writing of the ketubbah (the religious marriage agreement), which is observed today, thus protecting the wife during her marriage and after the husband's death. Also, the ketubbah was meant to discourage divorce.

* Mar Bar Ravina. He introduced a special addition to the Amidah (silent prayer made in standing):

My God, guard my tongue from evil and my lips from speaking guile . . . May the words of my mouth and the meditation of my heart be acceptable to you, O God, my rock and my redeemer.

He was also known to have smashed a glass at his son's

wedding. Apparently, it was done out of joy. We have seen earlier that another rabbi did the same, but the intention was to commemorate the destruction of the Jerusalem temples while celebrating the joy of a wedding.

* Rabbi Meir. Also known as Rabbi Meir Baal Hanness (Man of Miracles). He is considered a legend in regard to Jewish tradition and rituals. He encouraged his generation and following generations to make one hundred blessings each day. This is the reason that the second-century rabbis and subsequent rabbis introduced a blessing for each event or action done by an observant person. In today's synagogues and homes, people pray for washing hands, putting on the tallit (prayers shawl) and tefillin (phylacteries), eating bread, fruit, or even praising God for a natural

event like thunder, rain, dew, and more. Rabbi Meir left an indelible mark on Judaism as he was more than just a great scholar and an expert scribe. He advocated having a reasonable balance between business and the study of the Torah. An intense study of the Torah could make any man, regarding of religion, equivalent to a high priest.

We remember that Rabbi Meir was a student of Elisha Ben Abuyah, who became a heretic and left Judaism. Yet both men remained personally and intellectually connected. We also learned from a legend about Rabbi Meir that he was a son of converts to Judaism, and he may have been a descendant of Emperor Nero, according to the Talmud.

* Rabbi Nathan. According to the Talmud, Rabbi Nathan introduced the tradition of binding the hands tefillin on the weaker hand. It is natural to assume that left-handed people put on the hand tefillin around the right hand.

* Onkelos. He was a convert to Judaism and a student of Rabbi Akiva. He is very well-known in Jewish temples and educational institutions to have translated the Bible into Aramaic. By doing so, he

helped Hebrew scholars to clarify certain words or phrases in the Bible that were not clear enough.

* Rav Papa. Unlike most scholars mentioned in this chapter, Rav Papa was not considered as brilliant and learned in the Torah and its mysteries. He was, however, a wealthy businessman and a practical counselor on life, marriage, and human relations. Nevertheless, we find in the Talmud several interesting sayings of Rav Papa. We chose the following two sayings which are helpful in modern times. "If you let a quarrel stand overnight, it disappears by itself." The other saying is, 'In the house of mourning, it is good to keep quiet."

* Rav. He was also called Abba Arikha (the Tall Abba) because he was the tallest in his time. He was a student of Rabbi Yehudah Hanassi. They were both influential in their generation. Besides being the founder of the Academy of Sura and dealing with halachic and judicial matters, he introduced several things to prayer and Jewish tradition. For example, the bowing in the Amidah (silent prayer) when the phrase "blessed be God" is pronounced. Also, the following prayer, done in Rosh Hodesh (the beginning of the month) was also introduced by Rav:

May it be your will, O Lord our God and God of our fathers, to grant us long life, a life of peace, a life of good, a life of blessing, a life of sustenance, a life of bodily vigor, a life without fear of sin, a life free of shame and confusion, a life of riches and honor, a life in which we may be filled with the love of Torah and fear of Heaven, a life in which you will fulfill all the desires of our heart for good.

Two more important things in rituals were introduced by Rav: For the Rosh Hashanah prayer, he divided the after-Amidah prayer into three categories: Malchuyot (kingdom of God), Zichronot (remembrances), and Shofarot (the blowing of the shofar multiple times).

The other important thing he did is to arrange the reading of the Haftarah, a reading from the Book of Prophets that corresponds to the reading of the Torah on Sabbath and holidays. On repentance, he said,

May it be your will, oh Lord, my God, that I will not be sinning anymore, and

what I have sinned before you, erase
in your great mercies, but not through
bad suffering and evil diseases.

Another famous sayings about domestic life from
Rav was "one should be careful not to wrong his
wife for being quick to weep. She is easily hurt."
Finally, according to Rav, the study of the Torah
could bring about the rebuilding of the temple.

* Shemuel (also called Bar Abba, son of Abba). He
was a close friend of Rav and the head of Nahardea
Academy in Persia. He was a straightforward
rabbi who pursued justice, a physician, and an
astronomer. He followed the law of the land even if
the law was against its own brethren Jews. He was
friendly and courteous to everyone. He attributed
equality to all. He used to say, "It is forbidden to
deceive any man, whether he is a Jew or a pagan."
He also said, "Before the throne of the Creator
there is no difference between Jews and pagans,
since there are many noble and virtuous among
the latter." He even fought for the dignity of slaves,
and he did not hesitate to fight for their freedom.
Being also a man of science and medicine, he could
be living in our modern century where we all seek

equality between people no matter their religion or economic status.

* Shammai. He was one of the last pairs (zuggot) with Hillel being the other sage making the pair. We could say a lot about Shammai if we did not say anything about Hillel (see above on Hillel). While Shammai took the Torah facts literally, Hillel was more flexible and more liberal in his views. For tradition's sake, those Jews who are waiting for the Messiah to come, the House of Shammai would be the prevailing party. For now and following historic deliberations between the sages of the Mishnah, it is the House of Hillel that is being followed by most practicing Jews

* Shimon Bar Yohai. Rabbi Shimon left a remarkable impact on Jews all over the word in matters of mysticism, doing good deeds, dressing properly for the house of worship, and respecting one's neighbor and never causing him to be embarrassed in public. He also advocated praying for food around the table, discussing words of the Torah, and never interrupting a prayer, especially when reciting the Shema. His love for the Holy Land was combined with his devotion to God and was considered as an obligation of every Jew to dwell in the Holy Land.

Today, many believers and nonbelievers in Israel and throughout the world observe the pilgrimage to the city of Meyron in Northern Israel, where his tomb is located. Rabbi Shimon initially supported the study of the Torah first before having a worldly occupation. He ended up supporting both while maintaining that the study of the Torah always took precedent.

Rabbi Shimon was also a pragmatist. He said that the Romans, in his time, were building roads and bridges in the Holy Land, not to benefit the local population but to establish comfort for themselves. Rabbi Shimon's kabbalah has developed throughout the ages, and his name is always mentioned when delving in the study of this special science of mystical ways to find and understand God.

* Shimon Ben Eleazar. A student of Rabbi Meir, he left us the tradition of being tactful with your friend or relative when a tragedy or mishap occurs. For example, he said not to try to pacify your friend when he is angry. He also said not to try to console a friend when his dead relative or friend lies before him. When it comes to pledges, when one makes a pledge (for financial contribution) or a vow

(for promising to do something important), Ben Eleazar said not to interfere in that pledge or say anything to that person at the time of the pledge or the vow. This is something respected today in many temples. People contribute or pledge to their congregations without having told anything more than dropping their pledge in a box or a basket to be collected by the ushers.

* Rabbi Shimon Ben Gamaliel (Gamliel). He was one of the ten martyrs executed by the Romans. He left us with many important sayings, but his most important advice is "observing silence is equaled to wisdom." This also implies that it is only advisable to say something important after deep reflection. Also, the practice of the Torah is more important that its study. Religious and nonreligious leaders around the world strive to observe the abovementioned two qualities: observing silence as necessary when it is times to talk, and practicing what someone preaches is more important that just preaching.

* Rabbi Shimon Ben Gamaliel II. When studying this tanna (mishnaic Jewish scholar) and president of the Sanhedrin just before the destruction of the second temple, we learned a few things we can

carry in our generation. Rabbi Shimon II has taught us the following:

- Tisha B'av fast is as important as Yom Kipppur. This implies that mourning the destruction of the two temples in Tisha B'av is not less important than asking for forgiveness on Yom Kippur.

- In his advice to be lenient and flexible in justice, Rabbi Shimon protected the right of wives and slaves.

- About modesty in erecting tombstones, Rabbi Shimon said that the wise words of the sages are their real tombstones, not their ornaments.

- Studying while young is a great advantage to education.

- The three things that are most important in this world are justice, truth and peace.

We hope this is what world leaders are striving for in order to fulfill Rabbi Shimon's advice.

* Shimon Ben Lakish (also known as Resh Lakish). Resh Lakish had a harsh beginning in his lifetime. The Talmud reports that he was a robber, a highwayman, and a gladiator for the Romans. However, when he met Rabban Yohanan Ben Zakkai, his life changed after he immersed himself in the study of the Torah, thus becoming a most revered scholar in Israel. We have learned from Resh Lakish the following:

- When one repents, it is important it is done from the heart (Resh Lakish repented, and consequently, his life changed).

- It is important that a sage should never become angry, and he should always fight evil inclinations.

- Scholars and students of the Torah should be exempt from paying taxes.

- A newly converted person to Judaism who has accepted all the rules of the Torah is more important than a Jewish person who was born with it, according to Resh Lakish.

- The Sabbath is so important that, according to Resh Lakish, it looks like a person who celebrates the Sabbath is given another soul beginning Friday evening as the Sabbath arrives.

- In modern times, the Sabbath is a special day as Jewish believers feel liberated from the chores of the week. Also in all synagogues and Jewish temples, converts to Judaism are warmly welcomed and absorbed into their respective congregations and communities with love and care.

* Shimon Hatzaddik (Simon the Just). He was a high priest of the second temple who lived three centuries before the Common Era. He was considered a man of miracles in the Talmud and even by Josephus the Historian. Simon the Just instituted certain rituals still observed today: the reading of the Kiddush (blessings over wine) and the reading of the haftarah (from the Book of the Prophets) on the day of the Sabbath and holidays. He also instituted the Havdalah (the blessing on Saturday night at the end of the Sabbath). Many sages after him followed the tradition he instituted according to which a man, rich or poor, must consume and make a blessing over four cups of wine on the night of the Passover Seder.

The Talmud reports that the name Alexander was added to the list of Jewish-born males in the year 333 BCE when Simon the Just met Alexander the Great himself and predicted that Alexander would be successful in his military battles.

Simon the Just is often quoted by yesterday's and today's rabbis for saying that the world stands on three things: the study of the Torah, service to God, and acts of loving-kindness.

We are reminded here that Simon the Just represented the link between the sages of the Great Assembly who received the Torah from the Elders (who received it from the prophets). Simon the Just handed the Torah to the pairs (zuggot) and the Mishnaic sages cited in this project.

* Rabbi Tarfon. He is mentioned in the Haggadah (the story of the Exodus, which is read during the night of the Seder) that he was so preoccupied with the Exodus that he and four other sages stayed up all night discussing that story only to be interrupted by their students who announced to them that it was already time for prayer (to read the morning Shema).

Like many benevolent people today, Rabbi Tarfon was extremely wealthy, and he helped hundreds of poor women get married so they could get their share of the tithe (meaning they could be helped economically).

He also associated the presence of women in a household to joy and stability. This is something that is acceptable in today's society despite some disagreements here and there.

He was famous in saying, "The day is short and the task is great . . . you are not required to finish the job, yet you are not free to withdraw from it."

This is something we can appreciate in our century.

* Yannai. He was a highly respected rabbi and a student of Rabbi Yehudah Hanassi. He was wealthy but humble, and his generosity enabled him to fulfill the commandment of charity. He not only helped the poor but he had also kind words to them.

This is what we learned from Yannai and could apply to our modern era:

- Charity must be done without embarrassing the recipient.

- A country under occupation must submit to the authorities.

The School of Yanai introduced some morning prayers that are still recited daily by congregants in all or most synagogues worldwide.

Although fasting days must be observed, Yanai made an exception to those who must consume food during their fast for health reasons.

* Yohanan (Bar Nappahah or the Son of a Smith). He was most revered for his Torah erudition and his knowledge and understanding of the Mishnah. He joins other rabbis for his humility, his generosity, and his compassion. The following are the words of Bar Nappahah, which inspired one of the morning prayers recited daily in most synagogues worldwide:

> There are six things, the fruit of which man eats in this world as the principal remains for himself in the world to come: Hospitality to strangers, visiting the sick, concentration in prayer, rising early to attend the house of study, raising children in the study of the

Torah, and judging everyone according
to his merit.

Through years and centuries, the same words were supplemented by other words of prayer and were included in the morning worship. For example: honoring parents, honoring a bride, attending funerals and escorting the dead, establishing peace between man and man and man and wife, and the study of the Torah is equal to them all.

Like Yohanan Ben Zakkai (next to be commented on), he believed in the power of prayers to replace temple sacrifices, which ceased to exist.

* Yohanan Ben Zakkai. Rabbi Yohanan should serve as an example in modern times when people need to face changes in worship or rituals. After the destruction of the second temple (70 CE), he was instrumental in prolonging the Jewish tradition and education by successfully exiting the besieged Jerusalem and establishing a new academy in Yavneh. He also made changes to rudimentary laws of the Bible. Perhaps those rules were not fully clear, but they were not deemed necessary. For example, the rule of making a woman suspected of committing adultery drink bitter waters was

abolished by Rabbi Yohanan. Most of all, he was a pragmatist, and in other ways, he was what we call today a gentleman and a scholar. He never cursed or mistreated anyone. He was an example of goodness and kindness.

No wonder that he found out that a good heart was the best thing a human being can have. When he sent out his five students to go out and discover what the best thing was in life, the students came back with different answers, but Rabbi Yohanan chose a good heart because a good heart included everything in life including a good eye and a good human character.

What we can learn today from Rabban Yohanan Ben Zakkai is the ability to adapt to reality and the desire to continue the tradition carried on by our forefathers. Education and study of the Torah saved a whole new generation and enabled the divine worship without the existence of the Jerusalem temple. In his eyes, God is everywhere, and God continues to exist anywhere we wanted Him to be within us.

A contemporary of Rabban Gamaliel II (head of the Sanhedrin), Rabban Yohanan Ben Zakkai influenced many scholars by seeking humility and never become ostentatious on account of knowledge of the Torah. Other sages who would agree with Rabbi Yohanan include Hillel the Great and Rabbi Zadok Ben Elazar who said, "Do not make the Torah a crown for self-glorification."

(For more information of on Rabbi Yohanan Ben Zakkai, see chapters 14 and 15).

In conclusion, the aforementioned scholars gave more emphasis to the Jewish heritage by introducing rituals and customs that connected Jewish worshipers to the Torah of Moses, thus making their prayers more meaningful.

Chapter Eighteen

Concluding Thoughts on the Survival of the Talmud

The following are short statements summarizing the main events encompassing the birth and the survival of the Talmud, which has been attacked by rival scholars (often Jews who converted to Christianity) and burned over six times in history by the local authorities, mostly Europeans. On the other hand, the Talmud, for most of the time, remained preserved in Middle Eastern and Arab countries.

* Among the most important Talmudists mentioned in the Mishnah and the Avot book was Hillel the Great, who simplified and modernized some rigid and complicated laws of the Torah, such as the laws concerning the end of the Jubilee (see above). The Mishnah and Talmud, at the time of Hillel, were not redacted yet. But they were intensely discussed among scholars, and their

principles were transmitted from father to son through rote memory.

* Rabban Gamliel I (Gamaliel I), head of the Sanhedrin, was the grandson of Hillel and teacher of Paul, according to the New Testament in the first century CE. The Mishnaic scholars greatly revered his wisdom and leadership. His death was considered a great loss for all the rabbis of his time.

* Gamliel II was the grandson of Gamliel I. They were both heads of the Talmudic academy.

As the original Bible influenced Christianity, it also influenced Islam. When comparing the Torah to the Qur'an in Islam, the Bible corresponds to the Qur'an and the Talmud to the Hadith (interpretation of the Qur'an accompanied by tales and legends).

* It is important to underline how the Talmud survived under Islamic laws while it was threatened under European rulers.

* The Talmud flourished in the seventh century and beyond under Islamic rule for many reasons including the fact that the Talmud and the Torah did not represent a threat to the Qur'an. In fact,

many laws of the Torah are observed in the Qur'an (including the dietary laws).

* In Europe, Justinian established harsh Roman rules in the Holy Land (527 CE). He established the code of the Roman Civil Law.

* In the ninth century CE, legislative codes were established jointly by Moslems and Jews under Shimon Kayyara and Moslem legislators under Haroon Al Rashid.

* Simultaneously, within the interfaith commission, the Babylonian Geonim produced what it called the Halakhot Gedolot (great legal codes) under the Moslem governor.

* The Babylonian Geonim established She-eeltot Uteshuvot (questions and answers). The answers were called responsa, which was equivalent to the Moslem fatwa.

* In 600 CE, Rav Huna and Ravah authorized an instant Jewish divorce without a cooling period of one year in order to prevent divorced Jewish women from marrying Moslem men, who were able to obtain immediate divorce under Islamic law.

* The Karaites in the Holy Land, just like the Sadducees, rejected the oral law and only believed in the precepts of the written Torah. While there was a constructive dialogue between the Pharisees and the Sadducees in the Talmud, the Karaite leaders were not involved in the mainstream Talmudic dialogue and debate.

* Saadia Gaon, head of the Talmud academy in Babylonia, rejected the Karaite opposition to the oral law and considered the Karaites apostates (928 CE).

* Saadiah Gaon had a great influence in the Hebrew circles, and he was instrumental in regulating and adopting the Hebrew lunar calendar. He was prolific in Arabic and Hebrew.

* When the Babylonian academies lost their influence in the Jewish world, the study of the Talmud shifted to Kairouan in the Maghreb (today's Morocco). Kairouan was a commercial city, and it served as an intellectual center for Arabs and Jews.

* Between 711 CE and 717 CE, the Arab armies completed the conquest of Spain and established Córdoba as their capital.

* During the eighth century, the Talmud and the Qur'an became the intellectual power in Spain under the Arab rule. The Academy of Córdoba was created.

* During the Golden Era in Spain, the following events took place: The Kairouan center for Jewish studies replaced the Babylonian academies in their influence over the Jewish world. From Kairouan, there was a direct postal communication with Spain, Italy, and to some degree, with some European countries like France and Germany where a small population of Jews could be found.

* During that Golden Era, Hasdai Ibn Shaprut, a Jewish scholar born in 915 CE, became an adviser and the top doctor in the royal court in Córdoba.

* The Córdoba academy progressed under Moshe Ben Hanoch who arrived from Baghdad (Babylon).

* In the eleventh century, however, Córdoba was destroyed by the Berbers who invaded Spain. The Jewish Center of Studies moved to Malaga, Spain, under Shemuel Hanagid.

* Lucena and Al Fassi were the next leading scholars. Al Fasi came from the Moroccan city of Fez to Spain.

* During the Golden Era, Jewish studies and the Talmud became available for the masses with the help of the abovenamed scholars and especially with the advent of Moses Maimonides (born in 1135 CE in Córdoba).

* Moses Maimonides was unique in completing several books that helped people understand the Torah. Among his most acclaimed books were the *Mishneh Torah* (a second interpretation of the Torah) and *The Guide for the Perplexed*.

* Maimonides was also known for his publication of the thirteen principles of faith in God. His work substantially helped the Jewish population worldwide in rediscovering their identity and pride.

*The thirteen principles of Maimonides also helped restore faith within the Jewish Diaspora. Maimonides, who was also a medical doctor and a philosopher, centered on the uniqueness of God and gave hope to those who had doubt about their faith. His point was that the presence of

God is everywhere, and it is up to man to obey the precepts of the Torah as it was given by God to Moses. There is also hope for the revival after death. This encouraged all those who read and studied Maimonides, Jews or non-Jews, that there is a world to come and that through good deeds in this world, we have a chance to continue living in a different form after our death.

* On the other side of the Middle East and Spain, the Jews of Europe encountered unbearable difficulty as some European monarchs did not tolerate Jews.

* When the Talmud and various Torah commentaries were introduced to England, France, and Germany, they were met with the resistance of the church.

* The French Edict of 846 was to remove Jewish children from their parents and place them in monasteries.

* In 942 CE, Sehok, a Jewish convert to Christianity, convinced the king of France to destroy the Jewish population. Furthermore, in 1007, the king of France ordered all Jews to convert or die. Since we do not have the exact details of the aforementioned edicts, we can only say that the Jewish population

of France was small and that details on numbers are not available.

* However in 1074, under Henry IV, the Roman emperor of France (not the French Henry IV, who signed the Edit de Nantes in 1598 CE), the small Jewish population had some peace and was able to pursue its tradition.

* The first Jewish scholar to reconcile the Talmud with European scholars was Gershom Ben Yehuda (960 CE–1040 CE). He became the first Jewish leader of the Ashkenazi population in Europe before Rashi. He lived in the city of Maintz, and he attracted scholars from Babylonia and other parts of the world.

* Rashi (1040–1105) was the student of Rabbi Gershom. He is considered as the most influential scholar in medieval times and the most illustrious interpreter of the Talmud and the Torah. Rashi's name derives from the full name Rabbenu Shlomo Ben Itshak. Thanks to Rashi, the Talmud was more understood. It created a certain rapprochement between Christians and Jews as Rashi could write in ancient French as well besides being knowledgeable in Hebrew and Aramaic. Consequently, in France

and in Europe, Christian scholars began talking to Jewish scholars. They realized that there is another version of the Bible from those scholars who knew biblical Hebrew.

* Rashi's grandson was Rabbi Shemuel Ben Meir (1085–1158), also named Rashbam for short. He was a leading expert in producing additional writings to the Talmud and Torah. Those additions were called Tosaftot. His youngest brother was Rabbenu Tam. They were both the best Tosaftists (authors of Tosaftot) in the Middle Ages. Both scholars represented the European Jews called Ashkenazim.

* In France, anti-Semitism persisted despite Rashi's enlightened way of interpreting the Talmud. Louis IX of France (1214—1270), more than a century after the death of Rashi, challenged the Jews to publicly defend the validity of the Talmud. A chief opponent of the Talmud and a converted Jew to Christianity by the name of Donin advocated the burning of all Jewish literature and conversion of the Jews to Christianity.

* The Jews were represented by Rabbi Yehiel of France. They naturally lost the debate, and all the

Talmudic books, written by hand, were burned in France in the year 1242 CE. We see here a deliberate action instigated by a converted Jew under a French king who was canonized as a saint. It is not clear if Saint Louis wanted to have the Jewish holy books burned, but it was clear than Donin, a converted Jew to Christianity, was responsible for this tragedy.

* In Spain, there was a similar situation that led to the Spanish Inquisition, a tragic ending for Jews and Moslems as they were expelled from Spain in 1492.

* Pablo Christiani, another Jew who converted to Christianity to become a Dominican friar in Barcelona, Spain, asked King James I of Spain to challenge the Talmud and debate a rabbinic scholar on the veracity of the Talmud. Ramban (Rabbi Moshe Ben Nahman) was such a man. The debate took place in 1263 and ended naturally in favor of the Christian majority even as Ramban was praised by the king and rewarded for a good debate. The Talmud was consequently burned, but the Jewish spirit and culture continued the struggle for survival, leading to the Spanish Inquisition.

* In 1483, Joshua Solomon Soncino of Italy and his grandson, Gershom Soncino, revolutionized the method of studying the Torah with the first printing of the Talmud, the Torah, and the Halakhah.

- As King Ferdinand V of Spain managed to reconquer Córdoba, the Inquisition in 1492 became a sure tragedy for all Jews and Moslems who would not convert to Christianity. It was the most tragic era for Jews who were given a choice to convert or be exiled from Spain. The chief inquisitor and executor of the Inquisition was the well-known Thomas De Torquemada, who is quoted in every history book as the person behind the Inquisition. The inquisition was also established in Portugal in the year 1536. It caused more tragedies for the Jewish population, as it did in Spain.

* As half of the Jewish population in Spain was forced to convert, there was some hope for the other half of the population to never give up the Jewish religion. Fortunately, Jewish learning and traditional rituals continued in other parts of the world.

* Yoseph Caro simplified the laws of Halakhah by being the first scholar to take credit for the Shulhan Aruch (see chapters 4 and 5). This pattern of a prepared table of laws was followed by several more scholars who wanted their followers to have a simple set of rules on how to observe the rules of the Torah and the Halakhah.

* In the fifteenth century, several Christian scholars studied the Talmud and the Torah. For example, Martin Luther (1483–1546) wrote *Sola Scriptura* in which he advocated that the Bible was the only source for belief in God. Conrad Pellican (born 1478 in Alsace) studied the Talmud. Christian Reuchlin was a self-taught Hebrew scholar.

* Throughout centuries Christian scholars wanted to know about the Jewish scriptures and the Jewish law. Some scholars used their knowledge of Jewish law in order to have a dialogue with other Jewish scholars. On the other hand, those scholars who hated Jews and wanted to destroy them also studied Jewish law in order to supposedly prove how contradictory the Jewish law was to the Christian religion. This was how the persecution of Jews through medieval times culminated in the Spanish Inquisition.

* Incidentally, thanks to Reuchlin, the Talmud was saved from being burned when another Jew hater, Joseph Pffefercorn, recommended to Pope Leo X to burn the Jewish texts. Fortunately, Pope Leo X read the works of Reuchlin and did not burn the Talmud.

* A bright spot in the history of the Talmud occurred in 1523 CE when publisher Bomberg produced a full copy of the Jerusalem and the Babylonian Talmud with commentaries, including those of Rashi, Maimonides, and Asher Ben Yehiel. The new edition served as a basis for dialogue between Christians and Jews.

* Unfortunately, after the death of Pope Leo X, the Talmud and Protestant books were burned under the new pope, Pope Paul IV, on October 21, 1553.

* Long before the Spanish Inquisition, Jews were exiled from England in 1290 CE. Several hundred years later, in 1665, Menasheh (Manasseh) Ben Israel lobbied for their return before Cromwell of England. Manasseh, who left Spain as a result of the long campaign of exiling non-Christians during the aftermath of the Spanish Inquisition, immigrated to Holland, which was a more welcoming state to

Jewish exiles from Spain. Manasseh was a prominent writer and a Talmud commentator, a Bible scholar, a passionate orator, and an enthusiastic lobbyist about justice for everyone, including for the Jews. After his death, the British government was set up to readmit the Jews to England as there was nothing found in the law of England that forbade immigration of Jews to their country.

* The new versions of the Talmud, written in the seventeenth century and before, were admired by European scientists and philosophers like Hobbs, Newton, Milton, and Ben Johnson.

* Other Jewish scholars made a difference in the world of religions and literature as they combined Talmud with science: Yehuda Halevi (1075–1141), from Toledo, Spain, was one of the greatest Jewish poets and philosophers of the eleventh century. His passionate love for the Holy Land, which was at war between Christian crusaders and Arab rulers, caused him to arrive there in a difficult moment of his life. He died there shortly after his arrival.

* Rabbi Isserles (1520–1572) wrote his own prepared table for the Jews of Europe, who are known as Ashkenazim. Thus, he completed the

prepared table originally written by Joseph Caro. The Maharal of Vilna, also named Rabbenu Loew (1520–1609), combined European enlightenment with a deep understanding of the Bible and the Halakhah.

* Baruch Spinoza (1632–1677) was considered the most prominent philosopher of the seventeenth century. His rejection of the validity of the Bible and of the Talmud caused him to be expelled from the Jewish community of Amsterdam. He was, nevertheless, acclaimed by most Christian philosophers of his century and subsequent centuries.

* The year 1648 was a bad year for the Jews in Poland. Under Bogdan Khmelnitsky, the Cossack Rebellion of 1648 killed many Catholic Poles and over 100,000 Jews in a region occupying today's Ukraine.

Poland lost three million of its population through territory loss. It was subject to several invasions during its history and, subsequently, to many tragedies that also took a toll on the residing Jews of Poland. As Poland was home to the majority of Jews around the world, it also suffered several setbacks and victories, culminating in the concentration of most of the Jewish population in the Pale of Settlement, which harbored some five million Jews.

* We all know the tragedy of the Holocaust and its outcome. Nevertheless, Bible and Talmud study thrived in Poland under several Jewish scholars—namely Rabbi Moses Isserles and Baal Shem Tov (1700–1760)—and the rise of Hasidim, and we can never forget Shalom Aleichem, the writer of *Tevya (Tuviah) the Milkman*, after which *Fiddler on the Roof* became a famous Broadway musical and a famous Hollywood movie.

* Another significant burning of the Talmud took place in October 17, 1757, in the Polish city of Kamenets. It was triggered by rivalry among Jewish leaders and Jewish converts to Christianity. It resulted in the burning of all existing books of the Talmud. The myth of the blood libel (accusing Jews of using Christian blood in order observe Passover rituals) was not believed any longer in the eighteenth century. The burning took place anyway, and it was authorized by the bishop of the church, Nicholas Dembowski. This tragedy resulted in an intensive rebirth of the Talmud in

other parts of the world and production of multiple reprints of biblical and Talmudic books throughout Europe and throughout the Ottoman Empire.

* In eighteenth-century Europe, Jews in Lithuania, especially in the city of Vilna (Vilnus), were led by the Gaon of Vilna, who was considered a Talmudic genius. He opposed the Hasidic movement, which rose in Polish Ukraine under the leadership of the Baal Shem Tov. Both leaders believed in the importance of the Talmud except that they differed in their approach to the holy book. The Hasidim (the Jews of the Hasidic movement) looked at the Talmud from what it was called a mystical ecstasy, while the Vilna Jews under the Talmudic scholars under the Gaon looked at the Talmud from an intellectual viewpoint. There was no violence between the two groups, but we can see here how Judaism in Europe was divided into two very different types of religious people who supported the Talmud.

* Next in history was the Ottoman Empire, which dominated a great part of Europe and the Middle East from the sixteenth century to the beginning of the twentieth century. In Turkey, false messiahs surged and confused the already-baffled Jewish

exiles who resided in the Ottoman controlled states, namely the Balkan States and Middle Eastern states like Egypt, Syria, and the Holy Land. Jewish communities in Greece and other Balkan states enjoyed relative freedom to thrive intellectually and religiously. Following the Spanish Inquisition, hundreds of thousands of Jews settled in Europe and the Balkan states. Cases of anti-Semitism were rare until the beginning of the nineteenth century when Jews were attacked by Arabs in Morocco, Tunisia, and Libya. In general, Jews were able to practice their religion and trade freely. The Talmud survived this time. Unlike in Europe, as seen above, the Talmud was no longer a threat to Christians, and it certainly did not represent a threat to Islam. The Halakhah was compared to the Sharia Law, and the Talmudic Aggadah was compared to the Hadith in Islam.

* One important thing occurred at the end of the nineteenth century. May 13, 1896, was a date to remember. Solomon Schechter, a Talmudic scholar from England, discovered ancient Hebrew literature buried in an ancient synagogue in the old city of Fostat, near Cairo, Egypt. This was called the genizah (a depository of sacred Hebrew

documents that could not be disposed of and were meant to have a proper sacred burial according to Jewish law).

Those hundreds of thousands of document revealed the lives of Jews and Jewish scholars since the first millennium. It was an important discovery that shed more light on the Talmudic era, thus showing the importance of the Jewish heritage, which was never lost.

* In concluding the Jewish intellectual and religious survival, the Talmud, the Mishnah, and the Bible with numerous versions and interpretations in multiple languages have made their way to every willing reader in the twentieth and the twenty-first century. Without any censorship or bias, the Bible, the Talmud, the Qur'an, and any other religious sources of study are available today in every library in the democratic world. When comparing today's availability of the Talmud to the restrictions found in the Roman Empire and the Middle Ages and beyond, one can only say, "Was it necessary to shed two thousand years' worth of innocent blood when the Talmud was to become one of the most eternal books, together with the Bible, in all its versions?"

Glossary

Aggadah—Aramaic translation of legend and folklore added to the Talmud

am haaretz—ignoramus; a simple person

Amidah—prayer done in standing and in silent devotion

alyah—going up to the stage in a temple to read a portion of the Torah

Amora—Scholar mentioned in the Gemarah

Ashkenaz—Hebrew word for *Germany*

Ashkenazi—Europeans Jews who developed their own tradition of the Torah

av—father

av beth din—second to the president of the High Court

BCE—Before the Common Era

Beitza egg—it is a tractate of the Mishnah

bava—gate

Bava Kama—first gate; first explanation

Bava Metziah—middle gate; second explanation

Bava Batrah—last gate; third explanation

beraita—outside source in the Talmud

bimah—stage in a synagogue or temple

Birkat Hamazon—blessing after the meal

Birkat Hakohanim—blessing made by the priests for the congregation

CE—Common Era

Dead Sea Scrolls—found in 1947, revealing life of the Essenes some two thousand years ago

drash—an inquisition into a text

eruvin—enclosure of two or more properties, allowing the faithful to walk on the Sabbath; size of two thousand cubits.

Gaon—a special scholarly title of excellency for the head of an academy (e.g., Sura and Pumbedita)

Gemarah—Aramaic explanation and commentary of the Mishnah

Guide for the Perplexed—written by Maimonides to help confused Jews who needed guidance

Halachah—the legal way in the Jewish tradition; literally, it means "a way to go" in legal matters

Kabbalah—mysticism (a deep way of understanding God); initiated by Rabbi Shimon Bar Yohai

Kiddush—blessing over the wine; communal reception over food and drink following a Sabbath or festival morning prayer (except for fast days)

kiddush hashem—sanctification of the name of God. This is said mostly on those people who died as Jews rather than accepting another religion or by challenging the authorities who prevented them from teaching the Torah.

Maimonides, Moses (1135–1204)—great philosopher, physician, and author of several books on the Torah

Midrash (literally meaning "search" or "inquire")—to understand the words of the Torah

mekhilta (means "measure")—to explain the book of Exodus

Mishnah—compilation of Jewish law edited by Rabbi Yehudah Hanassi into six orders

Onkelos—he translated the Bible into Aramaic (second century)

Qumran—the site where the Dead Sea Scrolls were found in 1947 (see Dead Sea Scrolls)

Shema—special prayer (Hear, O Israel) preceding the Amidah (see above Amidah)

Sfaradim—Jews descending from the Iberian Peninsula (Spain and Portugal)

sifra (means "book")—it explains the book of Leviticus

sifrei (plural of *book*)—it explains and makes comments on the books of Numbers and Deuteronomy

Shulhan Aruch—a prepared table originated by Yoseph Caro citing simplified laws to be observed

Talmud—it comprises the Mishnah and the Gemarah (there is a Jerusalem and a Babylonian Talmud)

Tabernacle—temporary holy site (made of tent structure in the desert) leading to the building of the first temple that was erected by King Solomon

tanna—scholar mentioned in the Mishnah (plural: *tannaim*)

taanit—fast

Tannakh—the Hebrew Holy scriptures: Torah (Torah), Neviim (Prophets), Ketuvim (Writings)

tefillah—prayer

tefillin—philacteries

terumah—contribution to the temple

Terumot—the sixth tractate in the Mishnah

Tisha Be'Av—the ninth day of the month of Av when both temples were destroyed on the same day of the Hebrew month (586 BCE and 70 CE)

Torah—the Holy Scriptures, including the Pentateuch

Tosephta—additional explanation by rabbis not included in the Mishnah

tum'ah—impurity

Zohar—work of mysticism (kabbalah); developed in the thirteenth century

Yalkut Yoseph—a prepared table by Rabbi Yoseph (in the manner of Shulhan Aruch) and written by his son, Rabbi Itzhak

yibbum—levirate marriage

Yoma—alluding to Yom Kippur

Yom Kippur—the day of atonement

Bibliography

1. *Jewish Law* by Louis Jacob. New York: Behrman House Inc. Library of Congress Catalog Card Number: 68-27329-1968.

2. *The Mishnah: Oral Teachings of Judaism* selected and translated by Eugene J. Lipman. New York: The Viking Press. Library of Congress Catalog Card Number: 72-12621. Copyright 1970 by the Bnai B'rith Commission. Distributed in Canada by the Macmillan Company of Canada Limited: SBN 670-47856-3.

3. *Everyman's Talmud* by the Rev. Dr. A. Cohen with an introduction to the New American Edition by Prof. Boaz Cohen. New York: E. P. Dutton & Co. Inc., 1949. No SBN or ISBN found.

4. *Akiva: Life, Legend, Legacy* by Reuven Hammer. Philadelphia: The Jewish

Publication Society, 2015. ISBN 978-0-8276-1215-0.

5. *Maimonides: A Guide for Today's Perplexed* by Kenneth Seeskin. West Orange, New Jersey: Behrman House, 1947 and 1991. ISBN 0-87441-509-8.

6. *The Works of Josephus: Complete and Unabridged, New Updated Edition.* Fifteenth printing. Peabody, Massachusetts: Hendrickson Publishers, 2000. Hardcover ISBN: 0-913573-86-8. Paperback Edition ISBN 1-6563-167-6.

7. *Six Memos from the Last Millennium: A Novelist Reads the Talmud* by Joseph Skibell. Austin: University of Texas, 1916. ISBN 978-1-4773-0734-2-11.

8. *Whose God Is It Anyway?* by Elkayam Asher. Elkayam Asher Publisher. ISBN- 978-125-774-5418.

9. *The New Testament, Hebrew Version.* Published and printed in Israel under the Bible Society of Israel, 1995. UBS code MR 273. ISBN: 965-431-00105.

10. *Abraham Geiger and the Jewish Jesus* by Susannah Heschel. Chicago and London: The University of Chicago Press, 1998. ISBN: 0-226-32958-5 (cloth). ISBN: 0-226-32959-3 (paper).

11. *The Passover Plot: A New Interpretation of the Life and Death of Jesus* by Dr. Hugh J. Schonfield (eminent translator of the New Testament and author of *Secrets of the Dead Sea Scrolls and Jesus: A Biography*). Bernard Geis Associates. Distributed by Random House in 1965 (Fourth Printing). Library of Congress Catalog Card Number: 66-22755.

12. *Pirkey Avot: The Book of Wisdom of the Fathers—a Mishnaic Masterpiece about Ethics and Social Behavior.* Written in traditional Hebrew and some Aramaic between the year 300 BCE and 200 CE. This book, which is a collection of principles from various sages who existed since the Torah was given, is quoted daily and weekly in Jewish prayers, and it is regularly read in its entirety three times each year in Hebrew temples.

13. *The Talmud—A Biography: Banned, Censored and Burned* by Harry Freedman. London, New Delhi, New York, Sydney: Bloomsbury Publishers, 2014. ISBN: 978-1-4729-O594-9.

14. *The Bible, the Power of the Word: And in Between the Lines* by Asher Elkayam. USA: Xlibris Corporation, 2008. ISBN: 978-1-4257-8562-8 (hardcover). ISBN: 978-1-4257-8554-3 (softcover).

15. *The Qur'an and Biblical Origins: Hebrew, Christian, and Aramaic Influences in Striking Similarities.* Asher Elkayam. Xlibris, 2009. ISBN: 978-1-4415-1180-5 (hardcover). ISBN: 978-1-4415-1179-9 (softcover).

16. *Entire Hebrew Text of the Holy Scriptures.* Tel Aviv, Israel: Yavneh Publishing House, 1979.

17. *New Testament* and author of *Secrets of the Dead Sea Scrolls* and *Jesus: A Biography.* Distributed by Random House in 1965 (Fourth Printing). Library of Congress Catalog Card Number: 66-22755.

18. *JPS Hebrew-English TANAKH (Old Testament).* The Jewish Publication Society, 2003. ISBN: 978-0-8276-0766-8.

19. *Daily Prayer Book and the Prayer* by Rabbi Adin Eben-Israel Steinholtz (written in Hebrew). Printed in Israel. No ISBN or year provided. Rabbi Steinholtz translated to modern Hebrew the Palestinian Talmud and the Babylonian Talmud and was awarded the Israel Prize for his edition of the Talmud. Also, he won, in 1986, the Marcus Award awarded by the Israel's president.

20. *The Book of Books of Islam* by Aharon Ben Shemesh. 2nd ed. Translated from Arabic to Hebrew. Tel-Aviv, Israel: Karni Publishers, 1978.

21. *The Holy Scriptures According to the Masoretic Text.* The Jewish Publication Society of America. Copyright 1917, 1095, 1955.

22. Current events and media including *USA Today, New York Sun, New York Times, BBC Network, The Guardian, Asian News,*

cable news networks and other media including *Time* magazine, *National Public Radio, Washington Post, London Times*, the internet, and Google.

23. *The Comprehensive Hebrew Dictionary* by Avraham Ben Shushan. Keter Press. Copyright 1974 by Kiriat Sepher Ltd., Jerusalem (including all biblical, Mishnaic, ancient and modern and scientific Hebrew terms and their grammatical etymology).

24. *Compendious Hebrew-English Dictionary*, Comprising a Complete Vocabulary of Biblical, Mishnaic, Medieval, and Modern Hebrew, Compiled by Reuben Avinoam (Grossmann). Revised and edited by M. H. Segal, the Dvir Publishing Co. Tel Aviv, Israel (year of publishing not available).

25. *The Koren Pirkei Avot* with translation by Rabbi Lord Jonathan Sacks and commentary by Rabbi Marc D. Angel. Jerusalem: Koren Publishers Ltd., 2009. ISBN 978-965-301-750-4.

26. *The Ethics of the Talmud: Sayings of the Fathers* by R. Travers Herford. 1971. Library of Congress Catalog Card 62-13138.

27. *The Authorized Daily Prayer Book.* Revised edition. Hebrew text, English translation with commentaries and notes by Dr. Joseph H. Hertz, the late chief rabbi of the British Empire. New York: Bloch Publishing. Copyright 1948 by Ruth Hecht, twelfth printing 1965.

28. *The Talmud.* The Steinsaltz Edition (Hebrew/English). Volume I, Tractate Bava Metzia, Part I. Copyright 1989 by the Israel Institute for Talmudic publications. ISBN 0-394-57-666-7.

29. *The Babylonian Talmud* (translated from Hebrew). Explained and translated by Rabbi Adin Steinsaltz. Masekhet Shabbat (Tractate on the Sabbath). Jerusalem, Israel: Copyright by Israel Institute for Talmudic Publications, 1969. (No ISBN available).

30. *The Heritage of Sepharadic Jews (500 Years After the Expulsion of the Spanish Jews)* by Dr. Adam Ackerman. Jerusalem, Israel: Good Times Publishing Company, 1991. (No ISBN available).

Index

circumcision, 22, 80

cleanliness, 161–62, 164, 173

clothing, 56, 176

code of Hammurabi, xviii

compensation, xix, 118–20

console, 218, 268–69, 309

consumption, xix, 32, 66, 76, 146, 182

contamination, 172, 174–78, 180, 183

courtyard, 126–27

D

damages, 118–20

David (king), xx, 1, 7, 257, 259

Dead Sea Scrolls, 276–78, 339–40, 345–46

Demai, 53

Deuteronomy, xix, 1, 8, 13, 52, 55, 57, 60–62, 64, 69–70, 108–9, 114, 136, 146, 204

Diaspora, 17–18, 20, 67, 85, 140–41, 293, 296, 325

divine presence, 189, 263–64, 293

drash, 13, 339

E

education, 222, 238–39, 262, 299–301, 311, 317–18, 360

Eduyot, 139

elders, xx, 90, 131, 191, 219

Eleazar (priest), 128, 192, 194–95, 216, 218, 223, 234, 245, 267–70, 290–91, 299, 309–10

eruvin, 81–83

evil eye, 261

exile, 10, 17, 224, 273, 337

exodus, xix, 12, 35, 50, 82, 86–87, 89, 93, 100, 264, 314, 340

Ezekiel (scribe), 93, 100

F

faith, 9, 186, 188, 222, 233, 278, 301, 325

false, 53, 215, 336

first fruit, 49, 53, 67–68

first issue of the womb, 144

food, 51, 61, 64, 82–83, 86, 102, 181–82, 290–91, 308, 316, 340

G

Galilee, 285

Ganzfried, Solomon, 32

Gaon, 14, 16, 323, 336, 340

Gemarah, xx, 11–12, 38, 41–44, 47, 94, 114, 135, 162, 195, 197, 255, 339–41

Genesis, 36, 204

get, 113

gift, 5, 65, 146, 149, 151

Gittin, 113

God, xvii–xix, 5–7, 63, 68–70, 91–92, 111–12, 148–51, 199–200, 204–5, 208–9,

Author's Biography

Asher Elkayam has been an avid learner of the Hebrew Scriptures since the age of seven. In his native French Morocco he was tutored by rabbis and scholars, especially Rabbi Reuben Ben David who was a great Torah scholar.

The author showed passion for the Mishnah and the Talmud and was widely exposed in elementary school to Pirkey Avot (the Wisdom of the Fathers), which is an important tractate of the Mishnah.

A former student of the Hebrew university of Jerusalem and Alliance High School in Haifa,

Israel, Mr Elkayam studied, beside biblical studies, Hebrew Morphology, Bible and Talmud.

He is the author of 'The Bible, The Power of the Word' The Qur'An and Biblical Origins', 'Love and Romance in the Bible' previously published books by Xlibris.

Mr. Elkayam studied comparative religions and previously wrote two books on the subject: 'Whose God is it Anyway' (to be found in Amazon.com) and ' Jesus Returns and Faces Moses'.

The present project reveals hundreds of wise lessons learned from the Mishnah and the Talmud which represent a clear explanation and interpretation of the Hebrew Scriptures.

Pirkey Avot is a masterpiece Mr Elkayam has been fascinated with for decades. He ardently shares his passion of that learned wisdom with the readers of this book. Those wise maxims can be heard in our century.

Mr. Elkayam is a multi lingual and multi discipline scholar. Besides his Hebrew, Bible and Talmud knowledge, he is also a French and Hebrew teacher, a graduate of the Political Science Institute of

Strasbourg, France, and a graduate of Towson University in education. In professional matters and as a US Army veteran he is also a graduate of the American Council of Audioprosthology (in helping the hard of hearing for the last 42 years).

CPSIA information can be obtained
at www.ICGtesting.com
Printed in the USA
LVHW04*1507300718
585376LV00007B/60/P